THE DRACULA COLLECTION

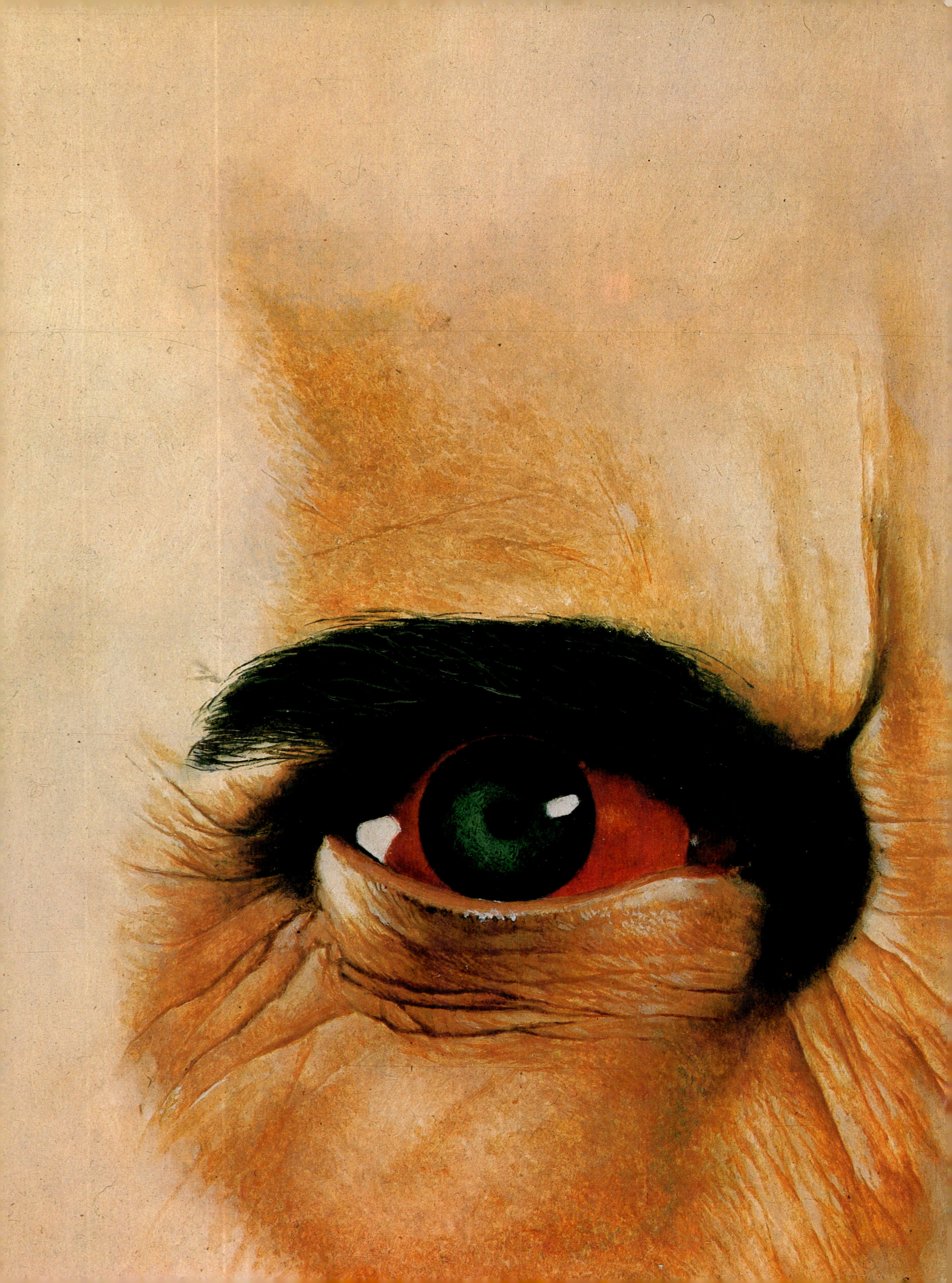

THE DRACULA COLLECTION

Selected Paintings from the Unique Gallery of
The Prince of Darkness

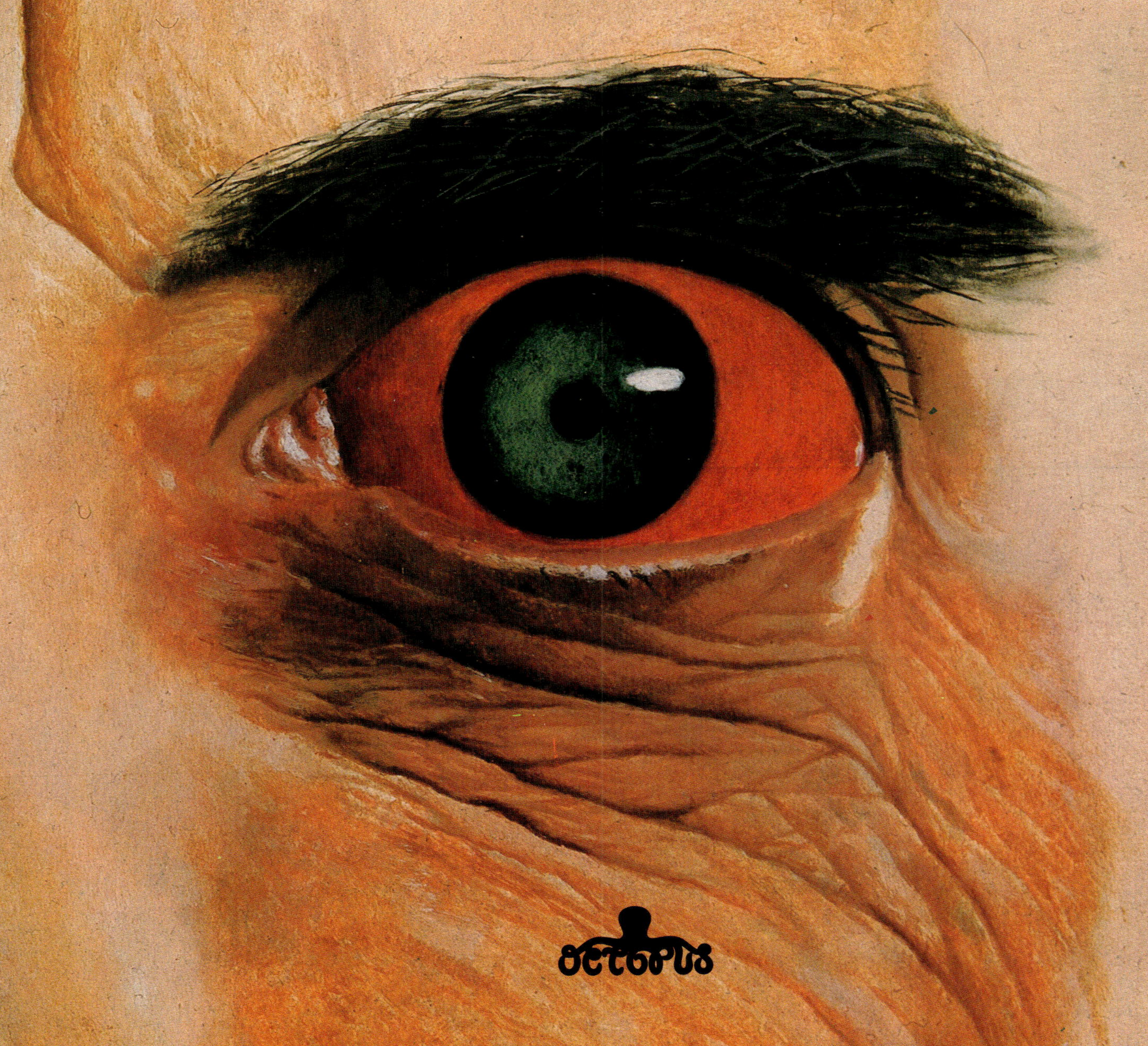

OCTOPUS

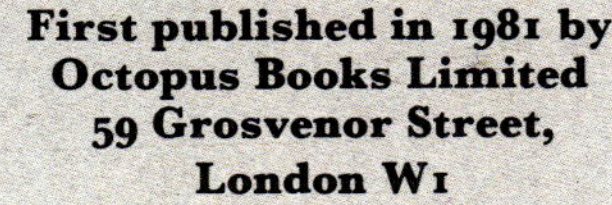

First published in 1981 by
Octopus Books Limited
59 Grosvenor Street,
London W1

ISBN 0 7064 1324 5

Conceived and designed by Cowley, Groom & Pickerill

Produced by Mandarin Publishers Limited
22a Westlands Road, Quarry Bay, Hong Kong

Printed in Hong Kong

Introduction

The publication of this extraordinary collection of writings is the final stage in a sequence of events that offers a glimpse into a dark and terrible world, the existence of which it is better to disbelieve. The path trodden by its unknown author leads from a dreary, unfrequented antique shop to the unhallowed citadel of one of mythology's most dreadful entities: Count Dracula.

In pursuit of his quest, the author intended to face Dracula on his own ground and, by doing so, placed both his life and his soul in the greatest jeopardy, with consequences that were almost inevitable. The dangers he confronted lay more in the supernatural forces he unleashed than in placing himself at the mercy of the notorious Count, and it was this unholy power that proved his undoing. Whatever his eventual fate, the surviving account stands as a most remarkable study of the world his host inhabited.

Through the verbatim record of his discussions with Dracula, we are afforded a first-hand impression of a terrifying environment. We learn much of Dracula's nature and background as well as his associations with other denizens of the occult dimension, and their place in that strange order. Such things nightmares are made of, but many of the revelations in this manuscript go beyond mere dreams to circumstances that, thankfully, the human mind can scarcely conceive.

Whether the author was courageous beyond measure or insane beyond salvation he has bequeathed to his fellow men the testimony of a madness that lurks a scant step beyond our awareness. Whether this account is an actual record of a terrifying expedition or the transcript of a fevered imagination, the horror it portrays will lie forever in the reader's mind; perhaps, through the dreams it engenders, it will open the ancient doors within to admit those things that lie on the darker side.

If you are resolved to tread the path beaten by the one whose hand set down this record, turn down the lights, close your door on the world and read on.

THE SEARCH BEGINS

What began as intuition became gradually an obsession and was later to come to fruition as the realization of my most consuming ambition, started in a most undistinguished fashion. My long and difficult journey into the most awesome realms of the occult had its beginnings in the dim and little-travelled alleys of East London, England. My long interest in supernatural matters had often led me to places that I would not otherwise frequent, but which offered me the possibility of furthering my already wide knowledge of the subject.

On this occasion, I had found a reference in an old and obscure paper written by a long-deceased student of the Dark Arts to a small establishment dealing in herbal treatments of a somewhat dubious nature. In addition to the mystical cures and remedies offered by its proprietor, ancient artefacts and curiosities were also available for purchase, many of which were of occult significance.

Inquisitive as to whether this establishment still existed. I made my way through the claustrophobic and foggy paths of the Isle of Dogs in search of it. It cost me several hours of impatient wanderings and fruitless enquiries before I came by chance upon a certain street. Something in the atmosphere urged me to investigate, and I turned into it, fully expecting another disappointment. To my great excitement, I had walked a scant twenty paces before I caught sight of a begrimed and poorly illuminated window over which hung a sign bearing the faded legend: Herbalist.

A sense of adventure rose in me as I pushed open the door and stepped into the gloom beyond. Scores of dusty glass containers gleamed in the dim light and all manner of dried plants hung from shelf and ceiling. As I gazed about me there was a soft footstep and a bent and grizzled old man appeared through a doorway. I began to speak of the quest which had brought me to his shop and enquired as to whether he had, for sale or hire, any documents pertaining to the occult in general, and vampirism in particular, which might add to my knowledge of such things.

He smiled a curious smile, came close to me and stared into my eyes with a most disconcerting intensity. 'You would have come some day!' he murmured after a long pause, 'Something in you belongs to the Darkness and you must beware its call.' Without further explanation, he beckoned for me to follow as he turned and withdrew from the room through a doorway, drawing aside the grimy curtain which obscured it. I did as he bid, aware of the thudding of my heart and the coursing of blood through my veins. Within was only darkness that seemed more profound than simply the absence of light.

I stood there, uncertain of where the curious fellow had gone and daunted by my total inability to see into the suffocating gloom. Stretching out my hand, I encountered the edge of a table or desk and stepped towards it. At that moment there was a flicker of a tinder-box, its small spark made brilliant by the lack of any other illumination. A moment later a trio of strangely scented candles flamed but to my astonishment they seemed unable to dispell the blackness and lit only the surface on which they stood. By their greenish light I perceived a scattered collection of ancient and crumbling tomes as the old man's voice invited me to sit and peruse them at my leisure.

At first I could comprehend little of their content, both the language and the profusion of mystical charts and diagrams were unknown to me, but as I stared at them in frustration, I found certain passages revealing themselves to me by some unfathomable means of which the eerie candlelight seemed to be a part. As I turned the fragile pages its elfin light seemed to linger on certain passages and the meaningless jumble of words seemed to make sense.

I hurried through the pages, most of which dealt with matters of more general occult wisdom, some of which I was already acquainted with. At last my eyes fell on a certain series of mystic formulae among which I recognized one dealing with defence against vampires. I was tense with excitement for I knew in my bones that I was about to take a further step in my obsessive journey of discovery: revealing the nature of vampirism and the plight of its sufferers.

I already knew as much as any man could of the history of this terrible phenomenon and the folklore with which it is surrounded and often obscured. My greatest desire and most persistent ambition has become the engineering of an encounter with one of the beings at first hand. Without doubt, the most celebrated and well documented of these creatures is Count Dracula himself, that legendary and feared citizen of the darkest corners of Transylvania.

Imagine my fevered excitement as I stumbled across a reference to his name in the book before me. It seemed to shimmer on the page in the unnatural glow of the candles as if itself animated by my response. My hands trembled and my breath caught in my throat as I urgently applied myself to examining the text before me. Much of the writings were little more than the usual warnings and historical references. However, I soon reached a portion of the text which was of far greater significance to me. It was clearly a description of the means by which the Prince of Darkness could be evoked. Labour though I did, however, I could make no sense of it; something hindered my understanding and the words refused to unravel in my mind as they had before.

In the utter blackness behind the shopfront of an obscure and little frequented herbalist's shop lay what was to prove the key to my remarkable venture into the supernatural world. A trio of strangely scented candles flamed into life to reveal a pile of ancient books.

It was then that I became gradually aware that I was being observed. Somewhere in the darkness beyond the lurid circle of candlelight in which I sat was something that held me in its intense gaze. I peered about me but could see nothing. Then, my heart almost stopped with the unexpectedness, a small shape leapt onto the table. I found myself held in the implacable stare of a small cat of almost oriental appearance, a stare that held in its depths the spark of a wisdom that should not belong in such an animal.

I could not look away, and felt myself drawn deeper and deeper into those magnetic, lambent eyes. I felt sleepy and uncertain. Dreamlike images drifted into my awareness and I could hear various passages of the text I had been reading as though spoken inside my head. One in particular was repeated many times: 'The Wild Ones who dwelleth among Men, yet are not of their world, are doorways to Otherness. Pass thou through them ye that are called if thou art desirous of it.' The realization that such a doorway had been presented to me stole through the misty turmoil that befuddled my brain, and I grew afraid.

Immediately, I felt the powerful attraction of the animal's gaze diminish and my mind grew more clear. 'For what other reason have I searched for so long and hard, or made my way to his dismal place, than to go where few have gone before', I thought to myself. 'At worst I have nothing to lose but my life or my sanity and they mean little enough to me'. Thus resolved I swept such thoughts and hesitations from my mind and let myself sink back into that peculiar lassitude once more. The creature's eyes grew larger and larger until they seemed to occupy my entire attention and breadth of vision. I felt myself falling forward into their dark chill as though tumbling slowly down the shaft of a well.

Unearthly sounds, smells and a distant keening wind distracted me and I ceased to know how I was orientated. Gravity had deserted me; I was not aware of either my own weight or my physical extremities and seemed to have become as smoke. Whether I became unconscious or simply slept I know not, but after an indeterminate length of time I suddenly saw a glow of light at what seemed to be a great distance. It was drawing nearer to me and the darkness all around me was full of indistinct movement and half-seen shapes. A foul odour assailed my nostrils and I felt nauseous; a growing sense of panic washed over me and I despaired of ever seeing the world I knew again.

I did not even know whether my eyes were open or closed but could see that the light I had noticed emanated from a particular point that was now much nearer, though I could not tell whether I had approached its source or vice versa. Whichever was the case, I was close enough to discern a curious figure seated beneath a delicate, intricate structure or pattern which burned with a blue light that was most unnatural. I saw no sign of movement to indicate whether the figure was a living being or merely an effigy bathed in that unholy aura. If it was the latter, it was extraordinarily well made in every detail. Within moments it was but a few metres from me, and there it remained as I fought to contain my unreasoning terror.

My attention was then distracted by an insistent whispering that increased in volume as I cast about me for its source. There was nothing in the roiling darkness to enlighten me so I could only assume that it emanated from the statue, if indeed that was the nature of the object before me. I could not, at first, distinguish any words in that sound, but gradually words emerged and I was able to detect their meaning. 'You are not of this place. Mortality stains you; treasure it and return, forego it and remain.' I stared at the image before me and knew that I could only travel further on this mysterious and perhaps fatal path.

Before I could reply to this unspoken message, I felt as though my intention had already made itself known, and as I watched, the bizarre figure receded silently until it was swallowed up in the almost tangible darkness. I was entirely alone once more. As I pondered my next move, I felt yet another pull at my awareness. I was as a small and insignificant piece of flotsam at the mercy of the tides and could only go where such forces willed. I surrendered myself to this new attraction, determined to quell my considerable fears and having chosen my course, make of it what I could.

Again I experienced that curious interval wherein I might have slept or passed into unconsciousness, but when I eventually awoke, I found myself at my original starting point; my head was resting on the pile of books I had been studying. Confused, I stood up, my legs trembling with the effort and perspiration springing from my brow. Was it no more than frightening dream evoked by the ancient wisdoms I had been reading and the mysterious atmosphere of my immediate surroundings? I felt at once both relief at being safe in the world I knew and acute disappointment that I was no nearer the realization of my quest than before.

As I pondered my situation, the trio of candles fluttered and died leaving me in total darkness yet again. Fear and anticipation clutched at my breast and I knew that the events that had transpired were no fevered dream. I stepped back from the table and the books that lay there, for whatever may occur would, I knew instinctively, do so there. Even as I stared in tense apprehension, a cold gleam illuminated the surface which pulsed and grew stronger. Though I did not witness its arrival, I found myself looking upon a most awful spectre. Seated beside those same volumes was quite the most terrible creature I had ever seen. Reptilian yet intelligent, neither man nor beast. An uncontrollable gargle of horror escaped from my bloodless lips as its eyes were slowly raised to meet my own, and I realized that my life was no longer my own to govern; other forces had me at their mercy and I had no resource.

As if in answer to a soundless command, I stepped weakly towards the being and looked deep into those terrible eyes; eyes that were windows into an unhallowed world that had existed long before puny Man had walked on the face of the Earth. As I approached I felt the air grow unnaturally cold and it seemed stale and scarcely breathable. I feared that my legs would cease to support me and I clutched at the edge of the table unable to turn my eyes away. Without a sound, the demon-thing placed its hand on one of the dusty volumes and opened it in a single movement. I looked down at the yellowed paper and the intricate diagram there revealed. I had no notion of what it signified, but I knew what was expected of me and placed the forefinger of my left hand firmly on a certain place within its complexity.

As I pored over the ancient manuscripts by the eerie candlelight, I felt as though I was under a most searching scrutiny. Looking up I found myself gazing into the eyes of a small cat, eyes in which gleamed an intelligence that did not belong.

At once the pale light, and the creature of which it was a part, vanished and darkness pressed thickly in on me. Almost as if seeking to cling to something familiar, I grasped the book beneath my hand and clasped it to me in trepidation. The air was unbearably cold now and I did not know how long I could withstand its icy chill. My strength was being drawn from me and I felt myself beginning to sway, when I noticed a faint sliver of light near the floor. I stepped forward to seek its source, my hand outstretched to protect myself against any obstacles invisible in the darkness. My fingers touched fabric and I realized that the light source lay beyond a long curtain.

Taking a deep breath, I grasped the cloth firmly and, after a brief pause while I collected myself, I wrenched the curtain aside. My scream died quickly in the thick atmosphere as I recoiled into the room, my arm over my face in defence against I knew not what. I had found myself immediately before a huge and awesome image; a black mask that was of no earthly thing. Noisome fluid dripped from its evil fangs and through its eyes lay empty space, an eternity of nothingness.

When at last I realized that this was no animate creature, my curiosity began to overcome my terror, and I recovered something of my composure. Returning to the extraordinary artefact, I peered through the gaping mouth, out into the featureless vista beyond. Mist swirled below a stone platform which projected from the base of the construction and I resolved to climb through. Feeling more certain of myself, I returned to the table and collected my portfolio and papers before ducking through the strange mask to stand on the ledge.

Once there I could see no more than I had from the other side; the dense mist so far below obscured any features from view. Feeling that I was meant to be here, I was sure that something would transpire and prepared to await events. My limbs were still weak from my earlier experiences and I turned to seek some comfortable place to sit. It was then that I perceived a rough flight of steps leading downwards from the platform towards the soft blanket of fog below. After a quick look around for any sign of life, I began to descend.

They were treacherously slippery and my progress was painfully slow. However, preoccupied as I was with the events that had occurred, I hardly noticed the passage of time and soon saw that I had left the platform far behind. The mist was only a few score metres below me and I pulled my coat around me in anticipation of its damp and chilly embrace. Some short while later, it was swirling around my ankles and, taking a last look at the open sky, I plunged into it.

My downward progress became extremely slow as I could only see each step with great difficulty in the cloudy gloom and the clinging moisture made each tread still more dangerous. I have no idea of how long I descended, but after some time the mist appeared to thin somewhat and my pace speeded up. Then with an abruptness that caught me unawares, I found myself at ground level. Tendrils of vapour still hung in the still, moist air but did not obstruct my view of a densely grown and swampy landscape interrupted by broad expanses of placid water.

I do not know what I had expected but it was not this strange place. The atmosphere was oppressive though not overtly evil but I was quite certain that this was not a portion of the world that I knew so well. Somehow my senses and intuitions were distorted as though in a state of feverishness; the things I saw and felt were 'wrong' in some way I could not determine. Even the foliage was disturbingly proportioned and colours were not quite as they should be.

As if seeking encouragement by reminding myself of the link with the world above me, I turned to look at the steps I had climbed down. To my great consternation they were no longer there. I had not moved far from them but they had entirely vanished in the undergrowth, and search though I did, they were nowhere to be seen. There was nothing to do but venture out into this clammy overgrown place and seek my fate.

A powerful sense of despair pervaded the air and seeped into my already depleted spirit as I walked over the spongy turf. There was a distinct lack of substance here and even the ground that I trod seemed insubstantial as though it were a raft of vegetation floating on the surface of some bottomless mire. As my boots pressed on its insecure face, they sank some way in and cold, brackish water oozed upwards from its body. I feared lest I suddenly placed my weight upon too thin a spot and precipitated myself into the depths. I had no means of taking my bearings; those plants which might have served as landmarks proved unstable in their very form, shifting and altering their shapes until they ceased to be what they had been. Colours too changed their hue and only the dank miasma remained constant.

Could this be some outer hinterland of Hell itself, a compromise between the world of flesh and the supernatural plane? I was now truly lost to my own habitat and I felt the animal stirrings of blind panic in my soul. I found it difficult to prevent a cry of desperate solitude bursting forth from my labouring lungs. I paused to compose myself, recognizing that surrender to such sentiments could lead only to madness, and succeeded in quelling my emotions. All my labours over these many years had been devoted to the pursuit of supernatural wisdom, so I could hardly resent the experience on which I was now so irrevocably embarked.

Thus fortified, I pressed ahead with renewed vigour and soon came to a dense wall of weedlike growth which I was force to pull aside in order to continue. Having forced my way through the clammy tangle, I found myself standing at the edge of a great expanse of foul-smelling water that stretched to the horizon. At this point I suddenly realized that despite the considerable time that had passed since entering the herbalist's premises, I felt neither hunger nor thirst. I considered this most fortunate as I had seen nothing that appeared remotely edible and I certainly did not relish the thought of availing myself of the noisome-looking waters that surrounded me.

In the furthest distance I could just make out the geometric forms of what could only be buildings on the opposite side of the lake. Lacking any other direction, I set off at once to investigate more closely. Progress was much improved as the narrow shoreline was free from the clinging growths that had impeded me earlier, and after an hour or more I could distinguish the distant structures more clearly. Alas, it was evident that they would obviously offer little shelter or solace, for they were obviously of great antiquity and in an advanced state of decay and disrepair. However, I continued to trudge around the perimeter of this dismal stretch of water

Over and over I tumbled through an infinity of darkness, jostling with half-glimpsed shapes and indeterminate movement. Finally I found myself standing once more, and a distant glow approached which resolved itself into a strange figure bathed in a blue, unearthly light.

towards the derelict settlement until I could distinguish its features clearly. I stopped to survey the mournful vista, and in doing so noticed that, on a fragment of masonry jutting from the rancid waters, a grotesque creature sat observing me. I can only describe it as a reptile in the approximate form of a man; a most repugnant and disturbing entity that was made all the more unpleasant through the impression of a sinister intelligence. Though different in construction, it was wholly reminiscent of the creature that had manifested itself among the books in the darkened room. Both were surely of no earthly origin.

We stared at each other for what seemed to be an eternity before the revolting beast emitted the gruesome parody of a laugh, slipped off its mossy perch and vanished into the stale waters with scarcely a ripple. Far from being terrified by its attitude and manner, I felt instead the stirrings of anger that I should be considered in such an offhand and insolent fashion by so base a being. Invigorated by my rage, I marched resolutely towards the delapidated cluster of buildings, determined to seek some termination of this purposeless interlude. I could not believe that whatever mystery had permitted me access to the extraordinary place would entirely abandon me to its cold and cloying airs.

Within a few minutes of arriving at my immediate destination, my earlier impressions were confirmed – the settlement had endured a great span of time since last it offered shelter to any living being or its creators. The massive stone blocks of which it was constructed were fissured and crumbling into decay and many lay tumbled from their seats. I peered through several of the huge window-like apertures only to find the dark interiors filled with all manner of horrid growths and fungi. I felt no desire to venture within and contented myself with clambering onto a precarious balcony in order to gain a higher vantage point.

For some miles around, the landscape was much as I had already seen; an endless mass of wet and slimy vegetation interrupted only by intervals of stagnant waters. Beyond this I could not see because of the ever-present mist that drifted among the taller plants. Wearily I sat down to consider my plight. I could see no return or escape from this desolate terrain and could not see how my access to it played any part in the search I had undertaken. Certain that I was no longer on the globe occupied by my fellow creatures, I could only guess at my position. Perhaps the supernatural world was one which existed in parallel to my own, in some other dimension of time and place. Occasionally one impinged upon the other to afford glimpses of life therein. If it was no more than this I bitterly regretted the foolhardiness that had led me here.

Hoping to divert myself from my unhappy musings, I looked at the ancient tome I had carried with me all this way, and idly turned the faded pages. To my astonishment, the text which had previously been indecipherable was now perfectly readable and I began to scan the pages with a mounting feeling of excitement. I do not know how long I sat there utterly absorbed in the weighty volume, for my attention was so gripped that I was unconscious of any distraction and oblivious to my strange surroundings.

Having been once more plunged into that interminable gloom, I found myself again in the small room wherein lay those mystic manuscripts. Suddenly, to my horror, a dreadful creature materialized among them.

VS EGRELLES

By happy accident, my eyes fell on a portion of the book which discussed at length just such a place as I now inhabited. Following a lengthy discourse on the separate regions of Earth and a supernatural kingdom of which Hell was clearly a part I read the following passage: 'And it was decreed that division shall be made between one place and another; that those that dwell therein shall have no supernatural intercourse, but each to their separate kingdoms shall adhere. On the one hand there shall be Order, on the other there shall be Chaos and each shall be lawful unto itself. It was further decreed that the two Places shall at no lawful point touch one upon the other and that there should be made another Place that is not of one nor of the other and that none shall have dominion therein. This Place shall be made of the four elements common to all Places and life shall be placed therein that shall not be instructed by either Order or Chaos. And so it shall be for all time and until the Day is Named.'

I knew at once that the place of which the book spoke was the very one in which I rested, and knew also that I

Above: **I wrenched aside the curtain and staggered back into the room, my hand outstretched to protect myself against I know not what. There before me lay the doorway into an unknown world.**
Right: **I pushed through the thick growths of serpentine, slimy plants and came to the border of a great lake. In the distance stood the ruins of a city while nearby a loathsome creature fixed me with its stare.**

would not be here at all but for some unearthly intervention. I was certain that my adventure was not over and that I had only to be patient. Though I continued to sit there for many hours, there was no change in the pale light to suggest that there was a night to follow this dismal day. Perhaps time did not exist here, which would explain why I still felt no need of nourishment. As I stared out across the unchanging and featureless vistas below me I began to find my predicament ludicrous, being little different from awaiting a tardy omnibus in a particularly drab and little travelled part of London.

My thoughts were becoming ever more self-centred when a flicker of movement among the vegetation bordering the lake caught my eye and I turned to observe more particularly. For a moment I thought it a product of my imagination until it was repeated. I peered through the moisture-laden air and witnessed a most extraordinary spectacle, for winding through the undergrowth was the most bizarre procession I had ever observed. A large host of reptilian creatures akin to those I had already encountered was making its way towards the very ruins I now occupied.

Uncertain of my reception should I be observed, I crouched back against the wall without losing sight of the peculiar assembly. One of their number appeared to be of considerable importance and was being carried aloft in a litter of some kind, with an air of nobility bordering on the ridiculous. I did not know whether to be amused or afraid and contented myself with watching from concealment as they wound their way among the derelict buildings and tumbled stones towards a small,

A host of reptilian creatures wound its way among the dense undergrowth in a bizarre procession towards the place where I rested. One of their number seemed of some importance and was carried on a regal litter.

domed structure that I had not previously noticed. Immediately upon their arrival at this point, they stopped and the regal being dismounted from its conveyance to stand before the doorway, surrounded by the unattractive escort.

I became convinced that the scenario below was for my benefit in some way and impulsively clambered down from my hiding place without hesitation. The creatures standing before the empty doorway seemed not even to see me as I approached and did not stir even when I passed nervously between them to the spot occupied by their leader. It was as though I was invisible. Encouraged, I walked to the aperture that was the focus of their silent attention and looked inside expecting the same scene of vegetable profusion that had greeted my previous investigations of such places.

I was not at all prepared for the sight that met my eyes. Instead of a convoluted mass of plant growth there was nothing – no floor, no walls, no containment of any kind. The impression of unending space stunned me and I clutched at the stonework beside me. I felt as though I was standing at the very edge of the world and was subject to the same eerie sensations that I had experienced when gazing into the eyes of the cat that had sprung onto the table in the shop.

I felt both dizzy and nauseous as my senses began to fail me and darkness crowded into my mind. Something was pulling at me, buffeting me and unseen shapes moved in the darkness before me. I felt myself passing into unconsciousness and my legs began to give way. I only wanted to escape from this dreadful doorway and began to turn away when my knees turned to water and I felt myself pitch forward into that terrifying void, falling yet not falling through a velvet darkness. It was as though I was suspended in utter emptiness where time itself had ceased.

THE DARK DOORWAY

I had no sense of my own body, as though I had become part of the temporal fabric of the void through which I tumbled. Tumbled or flew, for I could not distinguish how I moved through that emptiness; it was neither up nor down. It was as though my body had somehow been absorbed into the vacuum leaving only my mind intact. I felt the ebb and flow of unknown forces pluck at my consciousness, pulling me first one way then another while unearthly sounds and whisperings filled my ears.

Without any sense of the hours, I was but a single point, a single grain of sand in a vast and shifting desert, entirely at the mercy of scouring winds. I could have been drifting thus since Time first began and my earlier life was no more than a dream of no substance. Then, imperceptively, the darkness seemed to thin a little. The insistent and unknown voices grew more subdued and there welled in me a pronounced feeling that an event of great significance was about to take place.

I felt as thought I was condensing, taking shape and substance in the void, gathering the darkness into myself as I fell and I grew aware of a heavy thudding in my ears that I recognized as the passage of my blood. Suddenly there was pain and bright points of light which blazed and died leaving pale blue after-images until the darkness vanished in a red flare of agony that I could not withstand.

I screamed in the most awful terror a mind could suffer, pain beyond endurance, but even as I did so I became aware that the darkness was returning. Only this time I knew I was in a different place and in a more familiar form. As the sound of my own despairing cry died away I realized that I was standing on firm ground once more and more natural breezes caressed me than had done moments earlier. I looked around to find myself standing on a stretch of moorland only too familiar to me, being in the immediate vicinity of my own home. The many features which I recognized so well only made my recent experiences all the more extraordinary and, as the tension flooded out of me, I fell to my knees and sobbed uncontrollably.

Gradually I regained my composure and rose from the damp turf. It was nightfall as I began to walk wearily in the direction of my house, wondering whether my patient wife despaired of ever seeing me again; for as far as I knew weeks may well have passed since the day I left to look for the small shop in London. Presently, I could distinguish the distant lights of the house and quickened my pace. The air was cold, but I thought that its chill was due in part to other things than the season and could sense that I was not entirely alone in the somewhat bleak landscape of the moors. Though I looked about me incessantly I could not spy any other creature in the gloom, but the impression remained with me as I approached the welcoming lights of the house.

My man opened the door to me and to my astonishment expressed not the slightest surprise at my arrival but greeted me in his customary fashion. I could only deduce that however long my adventures had seemed to me, no more than a day or two had passed in earthly time. I even began to wonder whether the entire, alarming episode had been no more than a figment of my admittedly active imagination. Then with a jolt I remembered the battered and fragile volume that I still clasped in my hand and knew that this was not so. But was the adventure over so soon? Had I really endured all I had simply to be returned to my own house, or was this a brief respite in a much greater supernatural journey? I could only hope that the latter possibility was the case.

The rest of the evening was uncomfortably normal although my wife remarked, not unexpectedly, on my apparent distraction. I replied that the trip to town had been fatiguing and this explanation appeared to satisfy her. Of this I was glad as I had no wish to alarm her as to either my safety or my sanity. Although I still did not feel any hunger, we dined together nonetheless, and after spending a few moments together in the lounge afterwards, retired to our respective bedchambers for the night.

I felt tired but utterly unable to compose myself for sleep and instead lay fully clothed upon the bed to muse over the past events. Whether I did indeed drift into slumber I know not but, after an indeterminate period, I became aware that something was afoot of great significance. The room became uncommonly cold and I noticed a strong breeze where none had been before, which fluttered the curtain and tugged at my bedclothes. An oppressive atmosphere filled the room together with a powerful odour of stale air. I sat up and peered around the darkened chamber in anticipation but there was nothing to be seen.

Suddenly I experienced again that terrible feeling of falling or floating through unlimited space. I could no longer feel the bed on which I lay, nor my physical extremities, and I knew that I was once more on the road I had taken in that dingy, gloomy herbalist's shop. I felt both acute fear and great excitement as I struggled to retain my presence of mind. I could dimly perceive an area of slightly lighter tone in the velvet void which appeared to be approaching me at considerable speed, and I focussed my attention on it. It gradually took shape but I could not discern whether I was heading towards it or it was approaching me. Then I began to see more clearly and my eyes widened in horror at the appalling sight that was taking shape before me.

My vision was rapidly filled with the form of a huge many-headed dog of quite incredible proportions. Somehow I knew that it could be none other than the

Pain and terror beyond endurance wrenched a scream of utter despair from my throat as I fell through the darkness. Then, as my cry died away, I realized that I was once more in a world that was familiar to me.

Guardian of Hell itself, Cerberus. I struggled to move away from its malignant stare but was helpless in the grip of whatever force propelled me through this endless vacuum. I instantly regretted my foolishness in precipitating events of which I was so certainly not the master, and pleaded desperately with I know not what to release me from its grasp, but to no avail.

Soon the frightful beast towered over me and in that instant I saw that behind it lay two vast portals. One was considerably larger than the other and its depths reflected a lurid red glow. The other held only darkness, and after some time during which the beast silently surveyed me, I found myself drifting towards the smaller aperture. I halted before it and found myself corporate once more, although such parts of my anatomy as I could survey seemed somehow insubstantial. I stood on the sill before the opening and turned back towards the Great Hound, but it was no longer in sight.

Instead I saw a most unexpected scene. Below me lay my own house, a scant few metres away, and I found I could alter my viewpoint in a fashion reminiscent of a telescope until my own bedchamber appeared but a few feet away. Even as I watched, I saw the door to the room open and light flood in from a hand-held lamp. By its light I saw something on the bed which filled me with a sudden rush of horror, for there lay my own body dressed exactly as I had been. The eyes were wide open as if in terror but there was no light behind them; they were those of a dead man!

Then, worst of all, I saw my dear wife step into the room with the lamp in her hand, saw her lips move to speak my name and the gathering aspect of consternation at the lack of a reply. Her hand moved to her mouth and her eyes were wide as she placed the lamp on the bedside table and moved to the bed where 'I' lay. I could sense her fear vividly as she bent down, touched first my cheek and then my breast. She stood upright, backing away from the bed as her mouth opened in a throat tearing but, to me, soundless scream that went on and on until my heart felt as though it would burst. I knew then that I was lost from the world of men.

As I watched this macabre event, unable to turn my eyes away, the scene shifted and distorted as though viewed through water and my last sight was of my valet rushing into the room before the image faltered, then evaporated altogether. I moaned in pity for my beloved wife and for myself, a wondering spirit cut off from all I knew or held dear. Somewhere beyond this dark doorway lay my destiny and that path was now all that remained to me. I turned, hesitated at the prospect of that eternal emptiness, then stepped into blackness.

To my astonishment, I did not experience the fall into night that I had anticipated, but instead felt firm ground beneath my feet. I almost stumbled with the shock of it and stared in disbelief at my own hands as they moved to prevent my fall; I had somehow expected to find myself a ghost or wraith without physical substance. Instead I was as much myself as I had ever been, and was even dressed in the same clothes in which I had laid myself on the bed. I began to doubt my own sanity;

***Below:* What I was now I knew not, for my body lay far behind me in the house that existed in another place and time. Then, I saw in the black eternity a terrible shape: the Hound of Cerberus, the guardian of Hell.**
***Right:* As I watched from my unknown vantage point, I saw, quite clearly, my dear wife enter the room where my lifeless body lay. If only I could have spared her the agony of discovery.**

would I suddenly awake to find myself once more in my room? Somehow I thought not.

If this were a nightmare, it was one of such clarity and realism that waking life seemed far more dreamlike. I ignored the confusion in my mind and looked about me. I was in a most dismal place and there was a scent of corruption in the air so strong that I found it difficult to breathe. The landscape before me was barren and lifeless, broken only by the twisted forms of dead trees jutting out harshly from the twilight horizon. Snakelike tendrils of clammy mist writhed among the spiky clumps of coarse grass that was all that sprouted from the damp and stinking soil.

Something specific disturbed me and made my flesh crawl, but it was some time before I could identify the source of my uneasiness. At last it came to me. There was no sound at all; no whisper of moving air, no leafy rustle, not even the almost inaudible ticking of unseen insects. Nothing. In any place in the world, however barren or inhospitable it may be, there is always some tiny sound to be heard. But here there was absolutely nothing to suggest that I had not abruptly become utterly deaf.

This was probably the worst thing that I have endured since this miserable venture began and the full horror of my unrelieved solitude struck me. I cried out to God but knew that this was one place where He was not to be found; I had stepped beyond. Then, just as I felt that my mind was about to consume itself with rabid, hysterical fear, something caught my eye. A small point of yellowish light had appeared in the distance. It hung there without moving for several moments and I felt some attraction tug at my inner consciousness; some presence impinge upon my subliminal vision. I felt a positive tension in the atmosphere and knew that I was not, after all, entirely alone. But what would be here in this hellish place, I wondered, and began to be more afraid of NOT being alone than I could have imagined.

Suddenly the point of light began to increase in size at great speed and I watched with apprehension that soon became fear as I realized that it was not actually increasing in size, but was hurtling towards me at incredible speed. Before I could move from the spot its brilliance scorched my eyes and the terrifying image of some ungodly creature, fanged and hairy, filled my view. Still there was no sound. Less than a pace away, it stared into my face, its wicked snout wrinkling as though it was inhaling my scent. Then, as quickly as it had come, it vanished to become once more a single point of light. Suddenly that too winked out and the darkness was again complete.

After the apparition disappeared, however, I could sense that something had changed. The very nature of the darkness was altered as though now recognizing my presence. Even the streamers of mist seemed threatening, gathering in on itself as if about to take more substantial form. I imagined all sorts of nameless horrors lurking now in its cloak and felt as though all the latent energies of this godforsaken place were resentful of my presence and were awaiting an opportunity to spring upon me.

I could stand here no longer; I felt utterly helpless and vulnerable and resolved that any activity was better than this waiting. My limbs felt weak and frozen and my first steps were faltering and uncertain. It took all my will to place one foot ahead of the other, but I persisted and as I moved a little of my courage returned to me. For lack of any other objective, I headed in the direction that had been taken by my terrifying visitor, supposing that it must have had some destination in mind that could surely be no more dangerous than I felt my present position to be.

Alone in a desolate landscape, unlit by any moon, I edged cautiously through the darkness. Suddenly a point of light appeared and hurtled towards me. There was a blaze of brilliance and an image of a wicked snout, then it was gone.

My spirits rose with every step I took until I began to feel quite confident and determined not to fall prey to the madness that hovered at the outer edge of my thoughts. I was at least on firm, tangible soil, wherever it may be. If this was the supernatural world it at least had some qualities that were familiar to me. The air, though foetid, was air; the ground, though unpleasantly moist, was ground; and, unlike the growths flourishing in the first part of my mysterious journey, the grasses and trees that I could see in the murk were of a kind to be found in my own world.

Thus encouraged, I lengthened my stride and closed my mind to the vague doubts and fears that lingered there. Even as I walked I felt this whole place become perceptibly more solid and the darkness less complete. I thought that I could just distinguish clouds in the night sky and after less than an hour this was confirmed when they parted enough to permit a glimpse of a pale and unhealthy moon. Even after they had obscured it again, enough of its wan gleam remained to light my way through the desolate vista, and I continued with still greater speed.

When next I saw it I was cresting a low rise surmounted by a black cluster of the leafless, blasted trees that had been much in evidence throughout my walk. It slunk, as though ashamed of its sickly appearance, from behind its vaporous veil just as I reached the crest. I stopped, anxious to make the most of its presence to determine my route. The scene it revealed startled me, for there below my vantage point lay the unmistakable sight of a large and sorely neglected graveyard, the hundreds of crumbling and mossy headstones gleaming in the thin glow in a most unsavoury fashion.

I quelled the uneasiness which beset me and reasoned that where there are dead to bury there must also be the living from whom they were taken, and walked slowly down towards the rotten and collapsing wooden fence that marked the boundary of the cemetery. There I stopped to survey the dreary scene, then moved to where the nearest tombstone stood to see what, if anything, was inscribed upon it. There was indeed an inscription, but at first I was unable to decipher the words. Then I recognized that it was written in the Bohemian tongue – a language in which I had acquired, through my studies, a passable fluency. At least I was on my own world, I thought, and that realization gave me some comfort.

I turned again to the headstone to read the inscription more completely. After some difficulty due to its poor condition I managed to interpret the main passage which stated the following: 'From life in life to life in death is the one herein committed. May God have mercy on us.' I turned to another stone nearby and stooped to read that also. Here was written: 'Death shall not conquer so God protect us.' I found the use of the final plural in each case puzzling and walked some little way to yet another gravestone. Here I read: 'Life without life inhabits – God save us'. Again that unusual reference. I also noticed that no dates appeared on any of the tombstones that I could read which perplexed me greatly.

Remembering my more immediate predicament, I straightened up and cast my eyes round the cemetery in the vain hope that I would spy some building or path that might offer some suggestion as to the direction I should take. A graveyard is seldom far from habitation and I yearned to lay my eyes on some sign of living humanity. There was, however, nothing to suggest a route and I chose instead to walk around the perimeter in search of a track or road leading away from this neglected and dismal site.

As I walked I tried my utmost to ignore a feeling of increasing tension that seemed to press in on me. The very air was growing thicker and more foul by the minute, as though I was approaching some appalling open grave, the occupant of which had yet to dissolve into the earth. I slowed my step, fearful lest I stumble into such an obstacle in the dim moonlight, and searched anxiously in the gloom ahead of me. Before long the stench had grown so pungent that I began to gag and felt my stomach heave involuntarily at intervals. What in God's name lay in the darkness around me?

I stopped, wanting to find some direction in which to run to escape the hideous odour and as I cast desperately about me I suddenly froze. There, silhouetted against the pale horizon, was the unmistakeable figure of a young woman with a cape drawn over her shoulders. Relief flooded over me at the sight of another human being and I looked for the most direct path through the desolated cemetery to where she stood. As I searched among the tilting headstones a small movement arrested my eye. At first I thought it was a quirk of the moonlight, but as I watched, the stirring was repeated. My blood froze in my veins for I had seen the earth over one of the graves shift, small trickles of loose soil running down the sloping sides. The realization struck me like a hammer blow; the earth was being disturbed from BENEATH!

I fumbled for the rotting remnants of the fence and clung to it for support, unable to tear my eyes away from the horrifying spectacle. Then, as I watched breathlessly, I saw something push up through the clinging soil, pause as if exhausted by the effort, then heave again and recognized with awful clarity the ruined, decaying shape of a long dead hand. Like some terrible waking dream I saw it reaching upwards as though seeking to touch the mist-laden air as more of the limb came into view. Suddenly I saw another hand appear beside it and the damp earth began to cascade away from the questing forms. Then, with one terrible convulsion, something obscene erupted from the tomb and surged to its bandaged, rotting feet. There, distinct in the unhealthy moonlight, stood an animate corpse, the moist soil still falling away from its suppurating carcase. I looked again to where the young woman had been, and saw her there still, facing the hideous thing without any sign of dismay.

The two figures faced each other without moving, one fair one foul, until an eternity seemed to have passed. Then the girl made her way among the toppled stones without taking her eyes from the grisly creature, until she stood immediately before it. To my horror she reached out and folded the ghastly object into her arms and laid her head on its collapsing chest.

I do not know how long the three of us remained motionless, but after some time she let go and stood back, her eyes fixed on what remained of the corpse's face. Like some grotesque puppet, it lowered itself into the reeking earth and slowly vanished from sight once more; only the freshly turned soil suggested that anything untoward had taken place. After the last movement had ceased, the woman turned and slowly made her way back to the rickety gate that I could now distinguish.

At first I could only stare numbly after her as she walked away from the scattered stones. However, the realization that she represented the nearest thing to a living being that I had so far encountered drove my confusion from me. I could not bear to be left alone here and spurred by this thought, I ran, stumbling, round the boundary after her. I was terrified lest she escape me and fell many times in my headlong chase through the coarse and tangled grass. At last I felt a path beneath my feet and saw her outline against the scudding clouds ahead of me.

My breath rasped painfully in my throat as I lurched after her; I could not manage even the weakest cry to attract her attention. My brain reeled with the shock of what I had witnessed and the effort of driving my failing legs in pursuit of what I saw as my only link with the living world. Suddenly, through eyes reddened with the aftermath of terror and the physical effort, I saw her glance over her shoulder at me. Her eyes widened in horror, the whites showing startlingly bright in the fitful gloom, and her mouth opened in a soundless scream. I tried to call out to calm her fears but no words issued from my foam-flecked lips.

I moaned in utter despair as I saw her begin to run away from me along the rutted track. The thought that she might abandon me to this awful place spurred my flagging limbs to even greater effort and the distance between us began to close once more. My chest burned and my muscles screamed in agony at the effort and I was terrified that my strength would fail before I was able to overtake her. Again I tried to call out for her to stop but she only ran all the harder, constantly looking over her shoulder at me. Each time she did so I attempted to signal her to stop but realized that my flailing arms served only to alarm her still more.

As I ran, clods of soil that had adhered to me when I had fallen repeatedly in the earth earlier, fell away and made me appreciate what a fearsome sight I must have appeared to her. I felt a rush of anger that she should find me more terrifying than the hideous being she had so warmly embraced in that unhallowed cemetery and the rage lent strength to my exhausted frame. The gap between us began to close more rapidly and it was obvious that her own strength was flagging. She was beginning to stumble and seconds later I was upon her and her cloak was within my grasp. In a last desperate effort I lunged forward to seize the fluttering cloth, but in doing so lost my balance and the two of us fell headlong to the ground.

Weak and exhausted, her struggles soon ceased and we lay there like the dead, fighting for breath. At last I raised myself on one arm and looked at her frightened face as she stared, wide-eyed, at me. Still panting, I gasped, 'I'm sorry to bother you, but do you happen to know where Count Dracula lives?' She was silent for a moment, her breathing laboured, then she nodded and pulling up the sleeve of her garment showed me her wrist. Tattooed there were the words 'Transylvanian Tourist Authority – Registered Guide', and I knew that the final stage of my long search had begun.

Even as I watched from behind the jagged forest of ancient tombs, I saw the earth shift, then heave as though trying to disgorge its contents. Suddenly a hand, ruined and decayed, thrust upwards towards the place where the girl stood in silence.
Overleaf: **The door creaked ajar and I stepped inside. There, standing in the gloom, stood the creature I had endured agonies to face.**

PRIETO
MURIANA

Once I had arrived at Count Dracula's castle I remained there for several days without seeing my host, pacing the long corridors and exploring the warren of rooms, halls and chambers. One moonlit night, however, I sensed that I was no longer alone in this vast and ancient habitation and the tall, imposing figure of the man himself eventually entered the huge dining hall where I was seated before the fire I had made. He stood for some time in silent contemplation of me, an unnerving experience to say the least, but there was nothing threatening in his manner, rather curiosity.

After some time had passed in this manner, he came and seated himself opposite me, at which point I hesitantly introduced myself, without admitting either my intention or revealing the circumstances of my arrival here. He actually seemed disinterested in such matters in any case and was quite undisturbed by my presence. Despite his somewhat offhand manner he appeared entirely willing to discuss many of the topics I raised with him. Others he would simply ignore and I gradually gained confidence until I felt able to interrogate him quite freely.

Although I was quite clear as to my intention to study this legendary being, I was uncertain how I might direct myself to the task until one evening I remarked, by way of idle gossip, on some of the paintings I had observed at various points within the rooms. At once he became more animated; I had apparently struck upon a topic of personal enthusiasm which was to provide a basis for endless discussion over the next weeks. Indeed, I came to realize that his private art collection and his vociferousness in explaining its contents provided an excellent insight into both the man himself and the world he occupied. I decided to follow this approach and the collection of interviews recorded here are the result. All manner of studies hung upon the walls and I was able to classify them into certain subject categories which deal with various aspects of his history. This first part deals with the Count himself. Through the several portraits of him that I discovered, I found it was possible to gain a vivid impression of his own history, amplified by his personal remarks on each one.

Dracula This was the very first portrait that was ever made of me. I was a reticent child and particularly active. I therefore would not permit an earlier portrait to be made, though now I regret this. It is pleasant to have some reminders of such periods of one's life when, as the centuries pass, one becomes a trifle more sentimental and nostalgic. This particular painting was commissioned by my late father to mark my coming of age, and is one of which I am quite pleased. Looking at it now I can observe that I was rather a fine-looking youth, was I not?

Author Most certainly, and of noble bearing. Had you by that time acquired your, a-hem . . . er . . . certain quality? By that I mean were you of similar disposition to that of the present?

Dracula Was I a vampire? Yes, in fact I had been from birth. It was an inherited trait rather than an acquired one. My father passed it on to me, having been drawn into that state during his later years. I was, therefore, the first of my family to carry the seed from conception and was, as a result, a trifle doted upon by the rest of the family. It has been a source of occasional regret to me that I shall not myself be able to pass on the family inheritance directly for, as you will no doubt know, a vampire by birth cannot conceive in the natural manner but has to perpetuate himself through indirect means.

Author How soon was it realized that you possessed this quality? Did you resist it at all?

Dracula My parents did, I believe, anticipate it but if not, the evidence was soon forthcoming as I found little succour from anything but fresh ichor from the first. As to your second question, quite the reverse. It was, after all, entirely natural to me and I did have the example of my father to encourage me in acting upon my inherent impulses as well as that of several of our relatives.

Dracula Both these portraits were made during the early part of my Middle Period as I like to call it. My parents had both deceased by that time, events which caught me somewhat unawares for, aware of my own immortality, I had never thought to consider that neither of them enjoyed that advantage. My father's demise was particularly traumatic for me, being the first. The characteristics of vampirism do vary from subject to subject, and his trait was very specific in that he could only tolerate the blood of pure maidens. This is a constraint which I, incidentally, am not bound by. On this occasion he sadly misjudged the character of a young girl invited to the house for this very reason, and suffered the dire consequences of his misplaced trust the very next night. My mother was distraught and her profound sense of loss was reflected in her physical decline. Reluctant to lose touch with father she made a pact with the Forces which allowed her access to him. I must say that she makes a rather spectacular spectre as she is not only a fine-looking woman but was always very imaginative with a wonderful sense of style. I still see her from decade to decade, as she sometimes chooses to materialize in her old bedchamber.

Author Both paintings are clearly from the same period and have much in common in style and composition.

Dracula They were indeed painted at the same time and by the same hand. Both my parents were dead by this time and I had no representations of them in my collection. I therefore commissioned a Seer known for his artistic leanings to rectify this omission. Though he attempted to invoke them for several days, he was unsuccessful. Shortly before he was due to leave, he decided to execute one of me instead. The result astonished us both for my father's image appeared in the wet paint. After it was completed he decided to complete a second. This time it was my mother as a young maid who appeared. I was pleased, but the artist died.

Dracula A period of my life that I do not recall with much pride. After my parent's death I became something of a recluse and rarely strayed further than was absolutely necessary. I preferred instead to wander through these corridors reliving old memories and attempting to make my eyes grow red. A little trick I have now mastered perfectly. There were a lot of vampires about in those days, many far more potent than I was, and I must confess to having felt a trifle inferior in comparison. My parents had cossetted me rather too much and without their constant encouragement and admiration I felt less certain about my own abilities and supernatural prowess. I even became nervous about my ability to fly and, as it is an activity which requires complete commitment, I suffered a series of painful and spectacular accidents, before electing to forego this dangerous method of travel altogether.

My health began to suffer considerably and I drew as close to death as it is possible for an immortal to do. My excursions into the world beyond these walls in order to nourish myself were reduced to the barest minimum, and were certainly insufficient to prevent a marked physical deterioration from which I have never fully recovered. I began to acquire an appearance of age in excess of those years I had actually lived, as well as dandruff and horrid spots.

This situation could not have been allowed to persist; I retained enough strength of character to force myself to take a grip on the problem. Unfortunately, as it transpired, I went rather too far the other way and devoted myself to a life of such wanton excess that I threatened to do myself as much harm this way as I had avoided in terminating my previous life-style.

I became a positive glutton, swooping out over the Transylvanian hinterland and hurling myself at the neck of almost anything that moved. I became far too flamboyant in all I did, executing the most unseemly aerobatics with a verve that exceeded my skill. As a result, I undermined my standing in the supernatural community through a series of spectacular, if not admirable, aerial disasters. I was rarely at home, preferring instead to spend all the dark hours hunting, whether I required sustenance or no, and would regularly travel so far from the castle to find fresh pastures that I was often unable to return without risking being caught in the sunlight. The latter, as you will know, being particularly injurious to me and terribly, terribly bad for my complexion.

On these occasions I would be forced to seek refuge wherever I could – in old catacombs, vaults, caves and even the cellars of other people's homes. I shudder to think of the dangers I exposed myself to. It would only have taken one passing oaf to open a door or lift a lid and I would have been instantly reduced to a few handfuls of rather unimpressive dust. Having already experienced that fate once in my long lifetime, I have no wish to undergo that transformation again. It is too easy for a breeze or gust of wind to spread the stuff about irretrievably; I dislike having to wait for any number of years for someone to reconstitute me. It leaves too much to chance. There is always the danger that they might not have been as careful as they should have been in collecting me, and I materialize only to find certain portions of my anatomy quite dear to me are still blowing around the wastes of Transylvania.

Author If I might interrupt at this point. May I enquire as to how you pass your time in such a dispersed state?

Dracula Tediously. (Long silence)

Author I see. Pray continue.

Dracula My rather arrogant bearing during this era led me into all manner of petty conceits, this painting being one of them. Feeding is really rather a private business in my present view, yet I was rather pleased with my new-found confidence and technique, and commissioned the picture that you see before you. It shows a method I evolved myself in my excessive zeal, whereby I approach the victim from behind. This would only be of interest if you appreciated that subjects are rarely enthusiastic about the principle of nourishing a vampire and it is usually, if not always, necessary to subdue them by a focussing of one's will.

I used to practice, for months at a time, the concentration of my peripheral aura until it attained such intensity and controllability that I no longer needed to mesmerize my subjects in the conventional way, but could approach from any direction I pleased. The only drawback being that the state of physical tension required to concentrate that aura would, almost inevitably, inflict me with severe wind. It is a measure of my conceit that I used to endure that particular discomfort simply in order to demonstrate my skill, even when there was no audience to admire it.

Author's note This particular painting is the only one I could discover that depicts the Count as he appears at the time of writing. It was hung apart from the pictures in the main gallery and I only discovered it by accident during one of my perambulations about the confines of the castle. It was partially concealed by a velvet drape and was much neglected. The Count clearly disliked it and I was curious as to the reason.

Author I could not help but notice the single portrait of you in one of the upper corridors. It is a good likeness and I am afraid that, left in its current position, it may deteriorate before long.

Dracula Yes it will. (Silence)

Author It seems a great pity that such an excellent piece should be neglected.

Dracula (Silence)

Author If you wish I would be pleased to take it down and do what I can to restore its lustre. I have some small experience in such things and would consider it an honour to try and improve its lot as a small token of my gratitude for the hospitality you have extended to me.

Dracula Please don't trouble yourself.

Author I assure you it is no trouble.
Dracula Yes it is.
Author Oh no it isn't.
Dracula Oh yes it is. In any case its very heavy and firmly fixed to the wall. Besides I haven't anything with which to clean it and I'm saving all my bits of rag. Would you care for a game of five-dimensional chess?
Author's note I was so intrigued by the Count's reluctance to discuss the painting that after a suitable interlude, I raised the matter again in the hope that he, having soundly beaten me at the game of chess – a game, incidentally, that I cannot fathom at all – might prove more inclined to talk. The opposite, in fact, was the case. He seemed to become somewhat agitated. I persisted, fearful that I might overstep the mark, yet consumed with curiosity. Eventually, he sprang to his feet, stood before the fire with his back to me and spoke.
Dracula I dislike the painting Sir because that particular style of sarcophagus is embarrassingly out of date, and you force me to disclose that I cannot afford another. I have lived many centuries and my wealth is finite. (Turns and stalks out).

Family Dracula

The revelation that Count Dracula possessed a family should, perhaps have come as no surprise, but somehow I had always imagined such a creature to have been self-originating. It was later demonstrated that, in fact, theirs was a well-established tradition of vampirism which was both inherited and acquired. I spent some time, as a result, identifying those portraits which were patently of other members of his family, and questioning the Count as to their identity and history. The category which follows is selected to provide a glimpse into the nature of the Family Dracula. There are individual paintings which have not been included as the Count showed considerable reluctance in discussing their subjects. I can only assume that some degree of rivalry or feuding has, and still does, exist.

Dracula During my lifetime, I have had occasion to marry, though as you are aware, I do not at present enjoy the conjugal state. This painting represents one of my early wives, she was a woman of whom I was both extremely fond and almost constantly irritated by. She was vivacious, well versed in the social graces and had a taste for extravagant living. Contrary to certain rumours that have circulated, I am not, or rather, was not, a celibate and enjoyed the company of women in capacities other than as perambulatory meals. Isabella, for that was her name, was of mortal extraction, but since her death has acquired spectral status and is quite well known in certain parts.

Author The picture is unusual, can you enlarge upon it?

Dracula I take it that you refer to the treatment of her mouth. Her exuberant personality was often an embarrassment to me for she was prone to ill-considered revelations of our intimate life. There was no malice intended, but I regularly had reason to be displeased with her indiscretion. I eventually had her treated as illustrated and found that our relationship improved greatly as a result. Being of rather dramatic disposition I am sure that she was pleased with the result for she delighted to affect a delicious air of martyred femininity whenever we had guests, a role which I have heard that she still relishes. Though rather fanciful, the technique became something of a fashionable mode among wives moving in the more elegant circles and for a few years there were many adopting the same device. Isabella used to invite friends of hers who shared her enthusiasm for the fashion and they used to sit in one of the drawing rooms making mournful eyes at each other.

Author What happened to her in the end, for I assume that she no longer resides here with you.

Dracula You observe correctly. The latter part of our cohabitation coincided with the beginning of my reticent period and my reluctance to encourage or participate in social activities was at odds with her temperament. She endured the solitude for some years but eventually, encouraged by another current fashion for satanic pacts, cast herself from a precipice and entered supernatural life full-time.

Author Does she still manifest herself in this guise?

Dracula Yes indeed, and, I must add, has made excellent use of her condition. She has taught herself, entirely without instruction, to whistle through the impediment in a most eerie and becoming fashion. I witnessed it myself some several years ago at one of our rare family reunions.

Author Have you taken many to wife in your lifetime?

Dracula No, not many. Probably less than twenty as I recall. Almost all of these were in my youth when it seemed proper to adopt the marital condition. I eventually decided that this was not altogether convenient. If my spouse was supernatural, we often found ourselves leading separate lives anyway, and if they were also vampires we would find ourselves in competition rather too frequently.

Dracula The first of these paintings shows my brother Igor, a vampire a few years my senior who was a very positive influence on me and taught me a great deal about the business. I believe that my parents had very high expectations of him and hoped that he would lead the family into a new era of supernatural eminence. He certainly showed a considerable promise at the start with a flair for combining the traditional qualities of vampirism with certain highly original innovations. For example, he was one of the first to demonstrate his proclivities openly, instead of, as had been customary, regarding it as a secret and personal affair. He was really in the vanguard of a new generation of young vampires who were instrumental in altering, for all time, the popular image of the vampire as a solitary and ghoulish character, lurking in woods and cemeteries in order to feed his 'habit' in a clandestine and somehow seedy manner. He brought a certain self-respect to the business which it had previously

lacked. He was a flamboyant character. However, to my parents profound disappointment, he showed no inclination for the grooming as future head of the family that was planned for him. He left for Hollywood and has not been heard of since. His activities and influence here, however, really established vampires as leaders in the supernatural community and I owe him a great debt.

My sister, the subject of the second painting, shared many of his characteristics but lacked his cheery and egalitarian style. She was much more aloof and self-possessed and took after father in this way. Though very much an extrovert with a highly developed sense of drama, she nevertheless preferred a more stately and solitary way of life and death. I remember her best for her soundless 'swooping' as we used to call it. She was very disdainful about the act of flying and would only employ it as a last resort, preferring instead to glide at tremendous speed in the strictly horizontal plane. It was a device she learned from some of our spectral friends and she was always very impressed by its visual effect. I must say that, although I was disparaging about this ploy, and would accuse her of blatant exhibitionism, she presented a magnificently bloodcurdling effect when she would hurtle silently out of the darkness at top speed with a marvellous wide-eyed look of evil personified.

There were, of course, serious drawbacks. Her victims would often be so horrorstruck by her spectacular approach that they would perish on the spot before she reached them. As a result she would often return to the castle as hungry as when she had left for, as you may know, it is absolutely *de rigeur* to feed from a corpse, however fresh it might be. I believe she is now working the tourist areas of Bohemia, but I haven't had news of her for many years.

Dracula This painting is of someone very dear to me, and in whose company I once spent a considerable amount of time. I have not, however, seen him for well over a century. I believe that I first met Uncle Vladmir quite early in my youth, whenever that was, and recall that I was instantly attracted to him through his gentle good humour and sense of fun. He was, in fact, indirectly responsible for encouraging me to develop my ability to fly, when, in one of his frequent playful moods, he set fire to my cot. There have subsequently been many occasions when I have had ample reason to thank him for this inducement.

Looking back to the time when he was a fairly regular visitor to this castle, I suppose that he was actually something less than a perfect house-guest. He was often liable to arrive unannounced and his stays here would frequently be extended to a decade or more. At the time, however, I was seldom resentful of these intrusions, and even looked forward to his appearance with some impatience. I used to find it comforting to listen, in the twilight hours of the day when I had arisen, to his distant shrieking as he strolled contentedly around the grounds in search of earthworms. At least, from this point of view, he was quite easy to cater for as he required little else in the way of sustenance and this provender was certainly not in short supply. I was never certain how he managed to locate the creatures as he never carried any illumination of any kind, but on the occasions when I had accompanied as a boy, he exhibited an ability to pluck them unerringly from the soil.

The portrait in my possession was commissioned by some other member of the family, and I really cannot recall how it came into my possession. I have an idea that it was given to me many years ago by Uncle Vladmir himself in a fit of guilt about his then frequent visits here. It was actually painted shortly after a rather serious bout of excellent health from which, as you can see, he thankfully recovered without obvious ill-effect.

I am uncertain as to his origins, and indeed never thought to enquire, as he appeared reluctant to discuss his personal history. I believe, however, that he originally died in southern Russia at some time in the fifteenth century. He was better connected than most ghouls and was known to have consorted with a number of eminent demons who, on admittedly rare occasions, would accompany him on his visits here. Although it was so long ago, I remember the latter events quite well as they were marked by festivities of the like that has not since been equalled, much to the relief of others of my family who thoroughly disapproved of old Vladmir and his profligate ways.

I, myself, was still quite young then and found those nights rather more entertaining than the company of my more conspicuously respectable relatives. I am uncertain as to how I should feel now that I am older and more inclined to prefer my own company undisturbed by idle revelry, but I must admit to moments when I miss the spontaneous exuberance of his reckless parties. I do not know what has become of him since those heady days but I would not be entirely surprised to hear that he had gone to pieces long since, as he used to shed quite a few fragments of his anatomy even in those days.

Author Something puzzles me Sir. May I enquire as to what would have happened to him should he indeed have become fragmented?

Dracula I find your question a little surprising, but I assume, therefore, that it is something that you have not yet experienced. He cannot not, of course, perish in the mortal sense, for there was no life in him to extinguish. It happens, nonetheless, that one's corporeal form can, through accident or natural deterioration, disintegrate. In such an instance the primeval identity becomes a 'loose' spirit unable to govern either its movement or its physical nature. It is also quite often unable to act upon any physical thing unless it is, at least in part, of demonic constitution. Uncle Vladmir is certainly still around somewhere in this sense, but I shall certainly not see him in the form of which I was so fond.

Author He had, I take it, no demonic elements in his make-up?

Dracula Hell's Teeth, (laughter) Dear Vladmir did not have a single atom of it. I used to advise him frequently as to the wisdom of seeking some fusion with that realm but, despite his association with many of the major figures in that environment, he chose not to take my advice. No doubt he now regrets his lack of foresight, but there is nothing to be done at this stage.

Editor's note

It seems quite possible that Count Dracula experienced his first doubt as to the supernatural legitimacy of his guest at this point, hence his expression of surprise at the author's first question.

Dracula Olga Korska was a cousin but, being mortal, she has been dead for some time. I have heard that her spirit is still about but this is unconfirmed. She was utterly demented and a joy to be with. My aunt and uncle had been dead for some time when I first met her, and at first I thought she was boringly abnormal. As I came to know her better I discovered that she was as mad as a hatter after all and made up for her mortality by striving to become a first-rate murderer. She sold her soul quite early in life and worked with a number of excellent demons to commit a spectacular succession of heinous crimes – favouring the axe as her chosen instrument of retribution. She became quite expert at chopping and practised incessantly on mice, beetles and that sort of thing. She was, alas, cornered eventually by an outraged mob of mortals. In the struggle to capture her, however, she created the most spectacular carnage before being restrained and later hung. Her spirit still haunts her home town and terrifies humans taking their evening constitutional.

Dracula This is Olga's brother Boris, who was also as crazy as a coot, but unfortunately not in the lethal way favoured by his sister. He lacked her strength of personality and was actually, in my own view, a bit weedy. He had a very introspective sort of insanity and I believe that he probably felt overshadowed by his illustrious and adventurous sibling. He was, in fact, the very opposite of her in that he turned the sharp blade of his madness against himself, whereas she turned it quite literally against her fellow beings. From the very first I knew of him, he was inclined to wreak the most terrible havoc on his own body, and it was really only a matter of time before he inflicted himself with some dire injury. When he finally succeeded in putting out both his own eyes with an eggspoon, Olga clapped with glee and was so impressed with his subsequent appearance that she seriously contemplated doing the same to herself. Boris is still alive but seldom seen. I last heard that he had succeeded in amputating three of his extremities with a rusty penknife.

Dracula This is cousin Vanya of whom I have always been very fond, despite the fact that he is generally regarded by the family as something of a white sheep. He is a vampire as well but has never been very content with his lot in this respect. He upset the family a great deal when he decided to become a monk – a freelance one as no established order would accept him. The poor fellow has always found it difficult to strike a reasonable compromise between his chosen career and his vampirism and even attempted to satiate his physical needs, without having to impose them on an unwilling victim, by biting himself. He did, in fact, bring himself very close to extinction by acquiring a taste for his own fluids, and his solitary way of life prevented any of the family being aware of his gradual decline in health. When nothing had been heard from him after a few years his father decided to seek him out. He found him in a ruined priory in a sadly derelict state and managed to get him to kick the habit, although Vanya still wears it on special occasions.

Dracula Ah, this is Catherine, one of my great favourites among my relatives. Again a distant cousin, she is a delightful young ghoul who is a regular visitor here. She is of artistic temperament and has studied creative divination under the celebrated seer, the Oracle of Mount Albac. However, she has brought to this field something of her own invention: the Talking Head. Her ghoulish connections gave her the inspiration to devise a system of supernatural communication combining spiritualism and post-death awareness with the physically intact mechanisms of the human body. Her first experiments were less successful in that she endeavoured to use complete bodies salvaged from recent burials, but these proved cumbersome and inconvenient. After a series of experiments she appreciated that it was only the head that was required and began distributing them to a close circle of acquaintances. The result was a highly portable means of direct communication. It was less subject to the emotional and therefore unspecific vagaries of conventional telepathy.

Dracula Here we see one of the great figures of Transylvanian society: Pieter Karmanov. As long as I can remember he was a prime mover in supernatural affairs both within this land and abroad and is one of the few earthly representatives to actually sit on the Demonic Council of Hades. He was my mother's uncle and was a regular visitor to this castle before the decease of my parents. His visits were always grand occasions accompanied by celebrations of all kinds: The Meeting of Spirits, the Feast of Thirteen, the Dance of Lost Souls and a host of other significant and august festivities. He brought a tremendous atmosphere of importance to the castle and would frequently arrive accompanied by celebrities of all kinds. I remember one particularly exciting event when Beelzebub himself came with him for a weekend and my father held a huge party to entertain his distinguished guest.

Ghouls, vampires, ghosts and revenants came from all over the country to attend and, being rather too young to participate myself, I lurked at one of the windows overlooking the entrance to see the splendid company arrive. A constant stream of guests in their finest regalia flew, materialized, stalked and shambled up to the front door until I thought that all of supernature was there. I did not believe that the old castle could contain them all.

Inside the air was thick with the smell of brimstone, sulphur, corruption and the sweet scent of candles made from human flesh burning to light the scene. The sound was unlike anything I had ever heard or have heard since. A wonderful cacophony of wails, shrieks and moans reverberated throughout the building until I was certain that the entire fabric of these ancient walls would be shaken apart. It was very stirring indeed and I can still recapture that feeling of wide-eyed exhilaration I felt when I realized that I was part of this dramatic and colourful world.

To this day I do not understand how my parents catered for such a diverse and vast assembly. I suspect that father had spent weeks scouring the countryside for the necessary supplies. For those of our king alone, I recall carriage-load after carriage-load of maidens being shipped in. I cannot imagine how he managed to find so many in such a short space of time. In addition there were crates upon crates of corpses of all vintages including, I remember, an almost unique delicacy: the remains of a medieval abbot who had turned to witchcraft. The delightful irony was that his very ghost was one of the guests.

Also in attendance were most of the leading seers and occultists who set up several communications booths where guests could contact any of their friends who were not actually present and a cartel of licensed minor demons organized a 'spontaneous haunting' facility for anyone who felt like a bit of exercise after one of the many sumptuous feasts. I, myself, was permitted to try this out under the watchful eye of my mother. Although it was an interesting experience, I remember deciding that spectral manifestations were not really my sort of thing. They are, after all, a somewhat frivolous pastime and physically uncomfortable if one is not existing on the purely spiritual plane.

Without doubt the most impressive aspect of the occasion was the guest of honour, Beelzebub and his demonic retinue. I could scarcely turn my attention elsewhere and can picture them to this very day. They remained throughout in the Great Hall, observing but not participating in the surrounding festivities. They appeared like a dark island in the midst of a tumultuous sea which swirled around them without disturbing their solidity. The space they occupied seethed with raw power; strange shadows danced among them and flashes of crimson light flickered in the darkness which seemed to surround them. The aura of unconfined evil which emanated from them was awesome and was something that I shall never forget. I think that even Great-Uncle Pieter was impressed by it.

Author What was his association with them and how did he come to be involved with them?

Dracula I am uncertain as to how he first began to play a major part in supernatural affairs, but centuries ago the Forces of Darkness were at the peak of their international activities. As their ranks were spread a trifle thinly throughout the world there were opportunities for laymen to take over some of the localized administrative tasks which is what Karmanov did in this region. At the time of the occasion I described, he was one of the Black Marshals for this country, a sort of supernatural magistrate or governor.

Author Does he still fill this office?

Dracula To some degree, yes, but I believe that he delegates much of the work as he has advanced himself still further. He has dispensed with the body depicted in this portrait and is much more involved with international business.

THE CIRCLE OF TERROR

Many of the huge number of paintings in the Count's collection were not of members of his apparently extensive family, but were representative of other beings inhabiting his strange and sinister world. Many works had been produced before he inherited the collection and their subjects were unknown even to him. Of these there were a few whose origins could scarcely even be guessed at, their significance being lost for ever in the mists of time. Others had been instigated by him and were therefore easily explained.

Dracula This portrait, originally commissioned by my father, is of the last being to share this castle with me on a permanent basis. His name was Gantar and he was my father's man since long before I was born. With nowhere else to go after my parent's demise, I allowed him to remain with me when I inherited the castle. He was after all, more a part of it than I was. I know almost nothing of his past before he entered service with my father, and indeed, I doubt whether my father was better informed. Gantar was old when I was a boy and I discovered that he was in fact a mortal of no discernible supernatural origins.

My father regarded him as more than just a servant and used him as an adviser on domestic matters, a confidant and ally, in addition to relying on him for the smooth running of the affairs of the household. In those early years, I was disinterested in his character or his background and regarded him as simply a fixture here that was as much a part of my life as the walls and floors. I wish now that I had been more curious and had enquired of my father as to what he knew of the man.

After my father's death and the dispersal of the family I inherited the estate, and Gantar came with it quite naturally. However, my inability to communicate with him frustrated my desire to know more of him. By this time, in any case, Gantar had been dead for some time, having expired during the course of a large, and for him hectic and strenuous, dinner party. I remember the event because I was impressed by the circumstances which struck me as being a masterpiece of timing.

In his secondary capacity as Master of the Cellars, Gantar had acquired not only considerable expertise, but a certain unreasonable possessiveness about its contents. My father had been content to allow him full jurisdiction in the selection and presentation of the wines – a responsibility which Gantar took most seriously. Though he himself imbibed no more than was necessary for the performance of his duties, he governed the use of the cellar's contents jealously. It was he who decided what was drunk when and in what quantity.

One day a particularly boorish party of my father's associates were staying. Though they were undeniably coarse and ill-bred they were particularly important to my father's affairs at that time and he was anxious to ensure that they were suitably entertained. At dinner, that evening, my father asked that his finest wines be served despite Gantar's protestations, and the latter, though acting as instructed, showed distinct disapproval throughout the meal. It was understandable in view of the disrespect the guests demonstrated for the rare vintages, preferring quantity to quality. Gantar became more and more enraged as the meal progressed until, at the end, when one of the guests requested that he take one of the bottles of my father's very finest vintage brandy to bed to clean his teeth with, Gantar, purple with rage, could contain himself no longer. 'Over my dead body' he cried clutching the last remaining bottle to his breast. Father, incensed and embarrassed, reprimanded him severely and ordered him to surrender the bottle as requested. Gantar did so with extreme ill-grace and promptly fell down stone-dead.

My father was so grieved that he commissioned a necromancer to animate Gantar's corpse rather than lose his services. By the time I inherited him he was in poor repair, and eventually collapsed altogether.

Author's note I discovered this painting on one of my rambles about the castle during the hours of daylight when the Count had retired to the vaults. I came across the room entirely by accident for it was a strangely situated chamber whose entrance was not normally visible. A peculiar twist in the staircase leading to the battlements concealed the entrance and I only found it when I noticed a very slight draught as I passed by. On entering, I found myself in a dim, circular vault lit only by a tiny slit of a window high up in one of the walls. In the centre of the floor stood a rectangular stone dias just a few inches high, the upper surface of which was inscribed with an ornate pattern which seemed vaguely familiar to me. On closer inspection I discerned that it bore some resemblance to certain diagrams I had noticed in the ancient volume that I had carried away from the herbalist's shop, though later, when I consulted the tome in the privacy of my room, I found that there was no representation of it.

A stone vase was set at each corner of the raised platform, though what they were intended to contain is unclear as they were empty except for a dusty residue in the base of three of them. The picture shown here hung on the portion of the wall opposite the door and was almost invisible beneath a heavy layer of dust and cobwebs. I disliked intensely the atmosphere in that chamber and only remained there long enough to wipe the surface of the painting clean to discern what lay beneath the grime. Despite the obviously quite considerable age of the work the colours looked almost as though they had been applied but a few days ago, so bright and crisp were they. The subject too was most unusual and I was anxious to learn something of it. I enquired about both the room and its contents that evening when the Count had appeared at his customary time.

Dracula I had almost forgotten about that room, though at one time it was almost the most important place in the castle. In my grandfather's era this castle was an important focus of supernatural energies at a time when all of Transylvania was swept up in a great conflict between opposing factions of the Demonic Council. During that terrible period there was considerable unrest in the Dark Regions and the dispute spilled over into this dimension and world. Some of the awesome battles between these opposed groups of fiends and demons took place in the physical world as well as the spiritual one with calamitous results for those dwelling in this land. The whole fabric of supernatural life was frequently disturbed, with quite innocent ghouls, spectres and vampires exposed to considerable risk as the whole fabric of time and space was occasionally distorted. Transylvania has always been important to the Dark Forces as a major gateway into the physical world and was bitterly contested.

My grandfather, anxious to protect the family against any demonic threat, intentional or otherwise, made a pact with the traditionalists in Hades to provide a safe Doorway that would not be known to the Insurrectionists, in exchange for immunity from the temporal changes that were occurring in the world outside. The agreement was negotiated and ratified through one of those demonic intermediaries known as the Black Magi, part demon part human, who are of both worlds but belonging to neither sphere of existence.

The one through which the arrangement was made was called Astrax Delta, one of the best and most powerful in the business, whose rank is the equivalent of the demonic Third Order. It is his portrait that hangs in that chamber and was placed there as a reminder to all travelling through that Gateway of the terms of the agreement and its authentication.

After the Uprising had been quelled and the usurping demons suitably disposed of, the chamber lost its importance and fell into disuse. For a while after the War, it was used on rare occasions as a short-cut for travelling demonic representatives, but has not been employed since before my father inherited the castle. I do not even know whether it still works, nor do I know of the whereabouts of Astrax Delta having not come across any reference to him since I was a very young child. I believe he had rather diminished in power and status by then as a consequence of rather over-stepping his authority once or twice. He was, I understand, a trifle arrogant in later years and considered himself rather more important than he actually turned out to be. The last I heard of him, he was reduced to exploiting his skills in settling minor disputes between demons and arranging holidays in the physical world for demonic dignitaries.

I suppose that I really ought to seal that chamber up as I feel vaguely uncomfortable about there being an access to this place from Hades to which I do not have a key.

Dracula This has always been one of my favourite paintings here. It was done by an itinerant artist of whom I know nothing and have never since heard of

despite his certain genius. To my great regret, the subject of the portrait is no longer with us.

Author Was she a close acquaintance, or is the picture in part a fanciful one?

Dracula On the contrary it is a particularly faithful record of the subject. She was for some years quite a celebrated figure in these halls, though her visitations were regretably infrequent. For many years she was wont to materialize at irregular, but always welcome, intervals in the manner depicted here. Once in a tangible form she was accustomed to drift about the rooms and corridors for some hours before disappearing from view once more.

I often attempted to communicate with her but without any significant degree of success. Indeed, she scarcely seemed aware of the existence of any observer. I say scarcely because there were one or two occasions when I did succeed in eliciting a gentle and rather enigmatic smile before she disappeared from view.

She fascinated me a great deal and for that reason I decided to commission the portrait that you see here. I was of the opinion that I was well versed in the nature of most phenomena in this, my twilight world, but I confess that I know nothing of her and suspect that she may well be of the future rather than the past or present.

Author Could you explain yourself a little further?

Dracula Certainly. There are many apparitions to be observed – spectres, ghosts, revenants and the undead in all their various guises – but their mortal origins lie in either the past or the present. It has, however, been known for temporal warps to occur which can precipitate a future ghost into an earlier time. The manner of this particular spectre's manifestation intrigued me. She gathers and manifests herself through a mist of fine particles, a fascinating technique which I have not seen employed elsewhere. Another spectre of my aquaintance was similarly impressed and attempted to duplicate the method. Though he began quite well, he succeeded only in turning himself into a rather unpleasant smear in one of the bedrooms and has resisted every effort to have him removed. He is also producing an unattractive smell. I'm afraid I have no idea what the horse-thing is, but the painter used to arrive on it.

Author This painting is unusual and, if I may be so bold, is a notably unpleasant one. Surely it is no more than an imaginative work and not representative of any particular event?
Dracula On the contrary, my dear fellow, it is not only a faithful record of an event, but the circumstance it so vividly portrays is at the very moment taking place in the vaults beneath the castle. If you so please, I would be quite happy to take you down there for you to judge for yourself whether or not the painting is accurate in its treatment of the subject.
Author Thank you, but I think I would prefer to forgo that pleasure. Please tell me more about the painting.
Dracula Although I am essentially immortal I can of course be terminated, at least my physical form can be. There are a number of ways this can be achieved, all of which are well known: a wooden stake through the heart, falling into running water, being exposed to natural sunlight and that sort of thing, but these accidents only destroy any material form. My astral presence remains unchanged until the opportunity arises for me to regenerate that outward form. My problem is that the latter cannot be achieved without the presence of the complete remains of my earlier form, retrieved from the circumstances which originally destroyed it – either the carcase, ashes or whatever alternative form it has taken.

There is obviously very considerable risk that such a solution is not possible. It may take centuries before pure chance allows a suitable opportunity to arise, and the odds are most certainly not in my favour, in which case I would be imprisoned in a spiritual no man's land: blind, deaf and dumb; death without death, an eternal dreamless sleep which I could not endure. In any case, the transmutation is itself a singularly uncomfortable experience.
Author How is this pertinent to the painting?
Dracula I apologise. I digress. The point is that there have been many mortals who have attempted to destroy me over the centuries with, thankfully, a notable lack of success. Some, however, have achieved their ends and I have had more than my fair share of good fortune in always being able to return. I am not a vindictive creature by nature, but cannot contain my fury as to the agony and misery I have suffered at their hands. Too often, retribution is impossible as they have been long deceased by the time I engineer a return. The painting you see here records one time when vengeance was mine.

The individual in question was a particularly irritating travelling cleric who wandered about the countryside creating difficulties for a number of supernatural beings and who was particularly troublesome for those of my kind. The humans living in this area had become a trifle restive and resented my excursions sufficiently to feel justified in contacting this individual in order to enlist his aid in curtailing my activities. I must confess that I underestimated his abilities and took little notice of his arrival and subsequent wanderings in the vicinity of the castle. To my eternal shame and irritation, he succeeded in duping me into believing that he was an 'undead', and a particularly charming one at that. So much so, that I offered him the facilities of the castle for a few days, during which time, by means of stealth and Concealment Rituals, he located my coffin and drove in a stake. I am sure that you can appreciate my rage at this deception. So arrogant was his character that he had the, for me gratifying, audacity to remain for some time in the castle, making free with my facilities and wine cellar. His greatest error was one of haste, for he had not entirely disposed of me, having failed to place the stake with the necessary accuracy although it was driven into my chest with such vigour that it penetrated the floor of the coffin and prevented my movement. The agony was indescribable but, inspired by my fury, I eventually succeeded in working the fixture free and was able to pluck it from my bosom. I then required only a day or two to recover myself and make good the physical damage he had so ungratefully wrought.

Once free and my powers recovered, it was only too simple a venture to make the required preparations and confront him. I found him inebriated in one of the passages and wrenched his life from him before he had even stirred. It was then easy to employ my powers to hold him in the twilight world between death and life and imprison him in the vaults beneath our feet. It remained only to introduce to his chamber one of Hades' mindless but objectionable elementals who does with him as recorded in this picture, subjecting him to agonies beyond comprehension, from which death cannot release him. So it shall remain for all time. He shall have Purgatory as his eternal inheritance and I have the painting to remind me of the satisfaction of retribution.

Dracula I appreciate your interest in this picture, for it represents one of my consuming interests: the breeding and culture of Hellbats. It is the only pursuit for which I have an unfaltering enjoyment and has endured over all the centuries of my life. I was first introduced to it by my father who was himself dedicated to the practice for most of his life and remains one of the greatest proponents ever to warm an egg. He considered it the only really acceptable hobby of a gentleman of breeding and his work in the field did much to establish the ancestry of the modern Hellbat.
Author Please forgive my ignorance, but I must confess that I am unfamiliar with the creature. Are they not a species such as I see throughout this building?
Dracula Indeed no, they have no parallel in the natural world and are unrelated to any other creature living or otherwise. I am somewhat surprised that you are unfamiliar with them as they are appreciated by almost every supernatural being, not only in Transylvania but throughout the world. I can only think that you must have enjoyed uncommonly good luck if you have had no need of them.

In their original, primitive form, they were distant cousins of a species of living creature known as the Vampire Bat, but carried within their composition a supernatural seed. It might be better to describe it as a facility for altering the flux of Time, which allowed them to move into another dimension, akin to the Fifth Dimension. It is a process quite similar to that of Astral Travelling and allowed them to escape physical danger by transferring themselves to the spiritual plane.

There are few beings in existence possessing a comparable facility apart from those associated primarily with the mystic realm who usually do not possess physical bodies. In the distant past, too distant for me to be able to furnish you with dates, certain mystics appreciated the qualities inherent in these creatures and used to employ them as spirits to the spirit world, but more importantly, made attempts to improve certain qualities in them through selective breeding.

This science fell into a gradual decline over the centuries for various reasons and the species themselves were threatened with extinction. Occasionally, mystics in various parts of the world conducted further experiments which helped to keep the art alive. Several hundred years ago, there was a resurgence of interest in the subject. My grandfather was in the vanguard of this revival and even wrote a treatise on the keeping and breeding of the creatures. His interest was echoed in my father, for whom it became a major hobby. His vigorous attempts to gain recognition for the sport elevated it to the position of an almost obligatory pursuit for the Twilight Nobility and there are now a large number of major breeders who compete very seriously in the production of champion examples.
Author I still do not fully understand what these strange creatures are used for. What form does the competition take and do they have any everyday applications?
Dracula The most important and usual application for these intriguing animals is still the one for which they were originally employed; that is, as messengers between the supernatural and physical spheres of existence. Certain breeds have been developed which are able to act as physical extensions of some purely spiritual beings who may wish to manipulate or act upon physical objects in this world. On the sporting side, there are many inter-dimensional races held, some of which attract entrants from all over the supernatural world with prestige and honour as the prize for the resulting champions. There are also a number of specialized breeders who concentrate on producing strains which have particular abilities such as Prediction, Event Manipulation and so on. There are several authorities in existence whose task it is to govern the activities of particular groups of recognized breeders and who issue licenses accordingly. I, myself, sit on some of the committees of such Boards.
Author Is this a painting of some of your own creatures?
Dracula Yes. It in fact commemorates one of my father's Hellbats. It was a supreme champion in its day which, after being withdrawn from competitive life, became one of the field's best-known studs. The chicks shown at the bottom of the painting were its first brood which all became later champions in their own right, one of which is still in my own stable.
Author What is the round object it carries?
Dracula It is actually only carrying it symbolically. It is to commemorate the day it won the Transylvanian Handicap, for which the trophy is the Orb of Nemesis shown here.

FOX

THE MUSEUM OF HORROR

I had been in the castle for some considerable time when I learned, through a casual remark made by the Count, that there existed, in the lower levels of his ancestral home, the remains of a macabre museum founded by his father and perpetuated by himself during the earlier part of his life. He admitted to a decline in his enthusiasm for it as time has passed and rarely visits it. When I expressed a considerable interest myself, he agreed to show it to me and, although the matter was not raised again for some weeks, largely because of my preoccupation with the gallery, I eventually reminded him and was taken into the depths of the castle.

To say that the experience was alarming cannot convey the degree of my terror. Although its contents were no more fearsome than many of the subjects represented in his collection of paintings, they were made more unsettling by being tangible. The most terrifying experience I faced was at the entrance to the museum which was guarded by the awful manifestation depicted here.

Dracula When my father first created this collection, a number of the exhibits were objects of great mystical potency which could have been most dangerous in the wrong hands. He therefore arranged for the elemental you see to be imprisoned at the entrance to deter all but those entitled to pass through. Part of the reason, I must confess, was that my father acquired, through somewhat dubious means, a number of items which should not really have been in his possession and the existence of which he preferred to keep secret. After his demise, and because my own interest in the museum was less enthusiastic, I chose to dispose of all the objects that were of a contentious nature, returning some to their rightful owners, if such was the case, and disposing of others of uncertain origins as best I could. I must have reduced the museum to less than a third of its original size, keeping only those objects in which I still had an interest or which had been of particular significance to my father.

There is now no real need for the Guardian that resides at this entrance, but my father bound him so securely that I do not believe that I could release him even if I so desired. He is, in any case, of some interest to me as he can often herald one of the psychic storms that occur from time to time by a marked, and usually vociferous, increase in agitation at his confinement.

Author What, pray, is a psychic storm?

Dracula You are fortunate indeed to have escaped personal experience of one. They are singularly uncomfortable phenomena for any dwelling in the supernatural world, wholly or in part as I do. They are accumulations of metaphysical energy in its most fundamental form which spill over from the region between the dimensions – an indeterminate factor from which most forms of both natural and unnatural energy is derived. On rare occasions, there are accumulations of such forces that cannot be introduced into the regular system at the appropriate rate or in the usual quantities. A build-up develops which is released at a certain critical point as an uncontrolled outpouring of raw metaphysical energy: a psychic storm. These seem to precipitate only in the supernatural environment, though for what reason I regret I do not know. Particularly vulnerable to these cataclysmic events are elementals, such as our friend here, and other primitive entities whose nature and identities are sufficiently ill-formed to avoid being swamped in the waves of undiluted energy that result from such an occurrence. In such a situation, the unfortunate being loses what little self-identity it may have and, in being reduced to unspecific energy itself, is dispersed into the general diffuse state. Hence my particular guardians agitation when such a storm is imminent. Fortunately for him, he is protected by the fact that his own existence is endowed with more than the usual degree of substance by having been made part of the very fabric of the castle – a fact for which he displays little gratitude. But these entities are never noted for their social graces.

These two heads were my cousin Catherine's first successful head-only communicators which my father purchased from her in order to lend his support for her new venture. I believe that both are in full working order and are certainly in excellent condition as you can see from their appearance. They are unique in being a matched pair for Catherine was usually only able to secure her raw materials in single units. On this occasion she was afforded the unique opportunity of acquiring the cadavars of a brother and sister who had been killed in some natural disaster.

I believe that her brother helped her obtain the bodies and assisted during the dissection and re-animation of the heads. Once my father knew of her success in adapting the twin heads for inter-dimensional communication he felt convinced that she ought to be allowed the opportunity to further her work in this area, and saw that the best way he could assist in this was to endorse the idea himself. Thus it was that he came to acquire the heads, with the intention of introducing the concept to as many of his august acquaintances as possible.

After a few trial demonstrations to several of his close friends, associates and members of the family, it transpired that there were a few difficulties left to iron out. It appeared that the two humans, whose heads now comprised her communications system, had not been overly fond of one another while they were living. A pronounced degree of residual antipathy existed between them and interfered with transmission and reception. At intervals the messages being relayed were garbled or even interrupted entirely as sentiments embedded in the consciousness of the two heads were stimulated by and impinged upon the energies or psychic vibrations being relayed through them.

Fortunately, one of the observers present during these early demonstrations was a necromancer of very senior status. He was sufficiently impressed by the results obtained, less than perfect though they undoubtedly were, to offer his

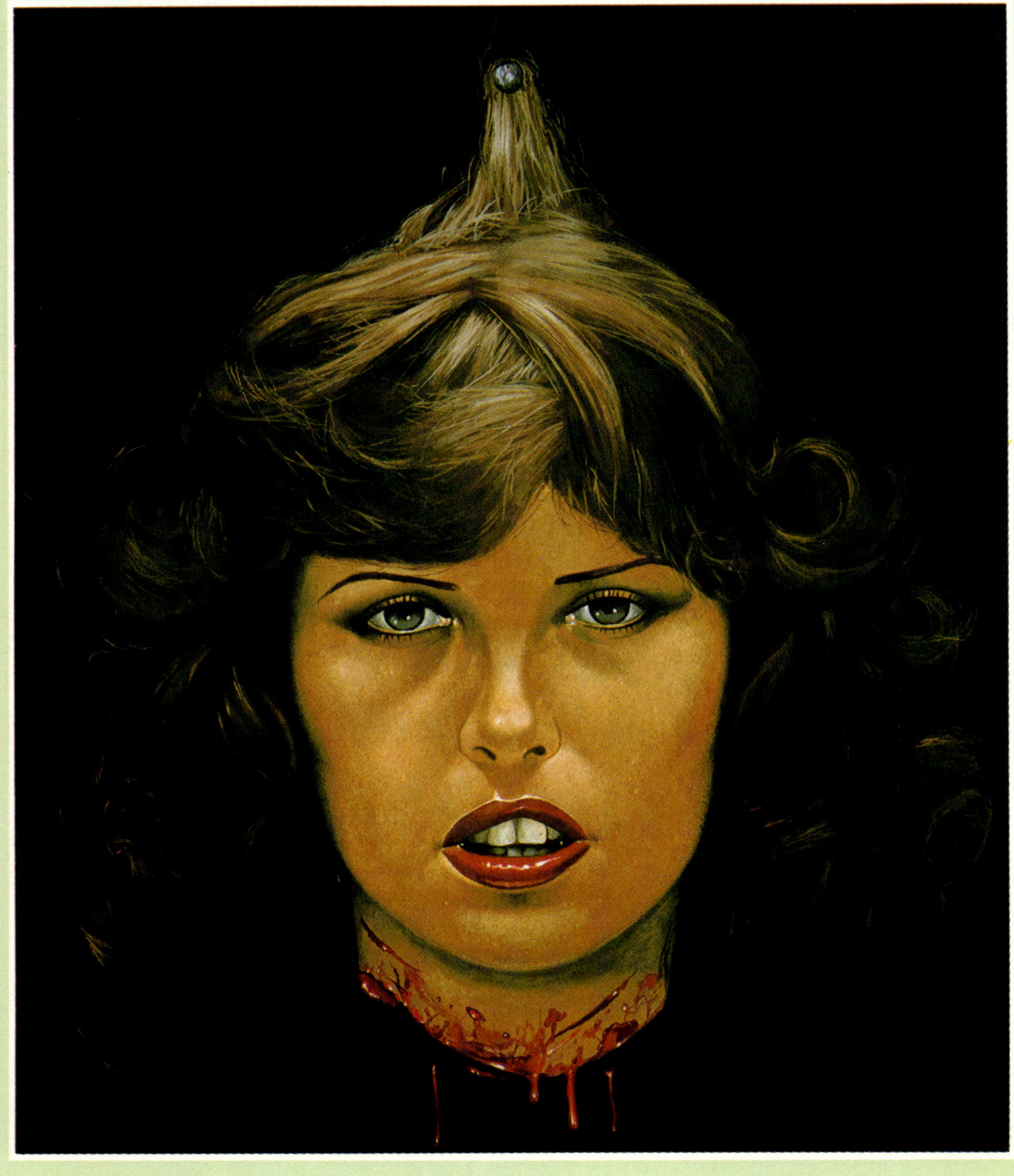

professional expertise in helping to improve their performance. My cousin was glad to make use of his considerable experience as her own knowledge of the field was strictly amateur. She learned a great deal about personality deletion and psychic cleansing as a result.

After having been subjected to the necromancer's skills, the functioning of the communicating heads improved enormously and reception was startlingly clear and free of peripheral interference. My father, now thoroughly impressed with their performance, decided to promote them more widely and offered to make them available for general comparison with existing media. It must be appreciated that this was a particularly generous proposal in view of the fact that the conventional method of inter-dimensional communication up until then had been almost exclusively provided by Hellbats. He was certainly one of the most progressive figures in the Transylvanian nobility and saw no good reason to stand in the way of progress simply because of his own vested interests.

In fact, speaking as one with intimate knowledge of his character, I am sure that his reasons for this apparently selfless act went further than purely family loyalty and encouragement. He had held the distinction of being one of the supreme leading lights in the Hellbat breeding business for some considerable time, and I think he was beginning to feel the pressure of keeping ahead of the new generation of breeders that were coming into their own. Catherine's new methods offered him an ideal opportunity to abdicate with honour from the prestigious position he had held whilst, at the same time, get in at the ground floor of a development which was very likely to alter the significance of Hellbat breeding for all time anyway. My father did possess a very strong entrepreneurial flair, allied to a shrewd political sense, and I don't think that I belittle his memory by such a revelation. Transylvania would benefit greatly if more beings of his ilk existed today.

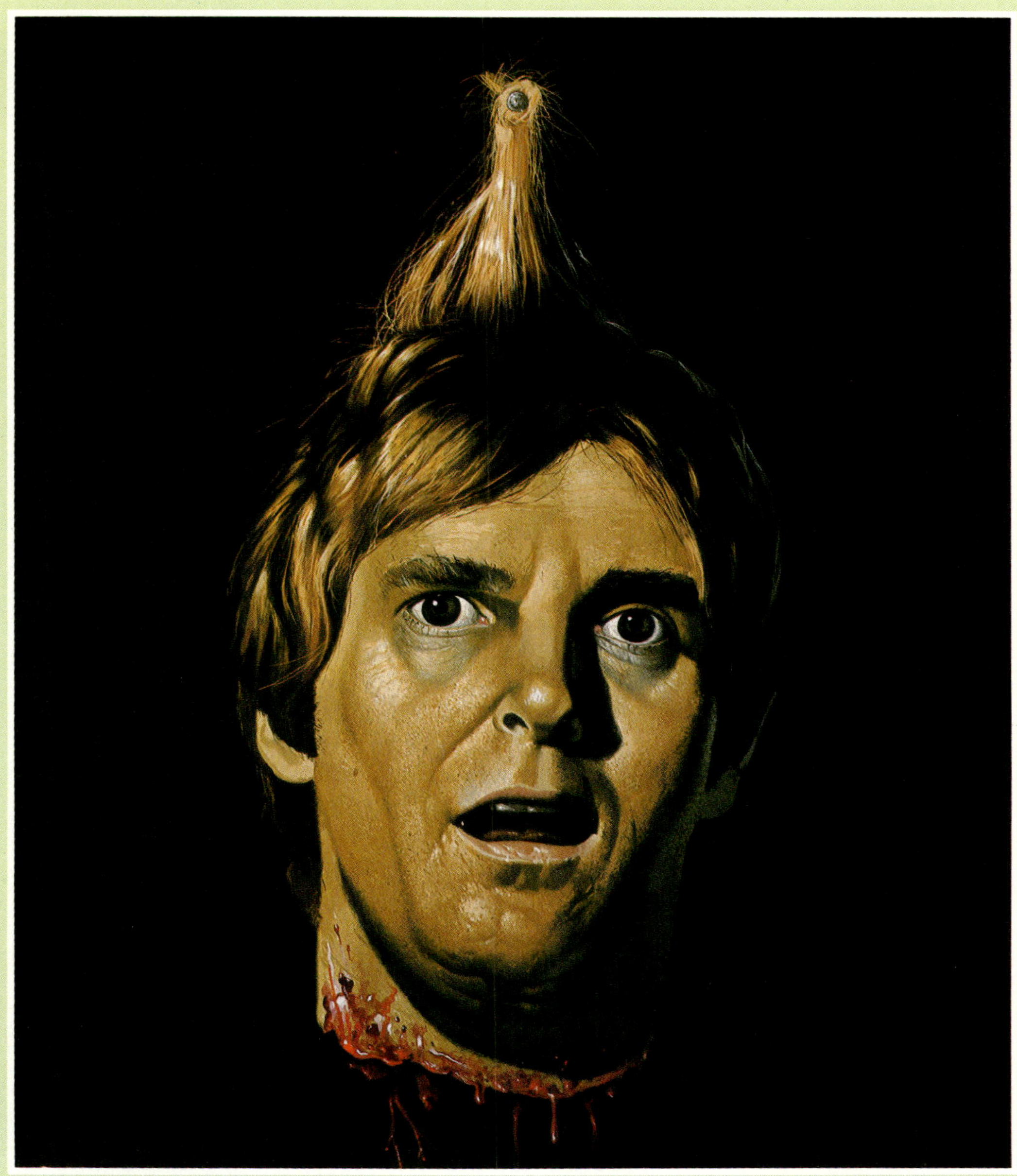

Author's note: As we passed through the labyrinth of chambers and vaults which had housed the collection of exhibits for unknown centuries, I could see that a huge number of items had been disposed of. There were scores of pedestals and niches which must have housed them but were now empty and submerged in a deep layer of dust and grime. Some of the objects remaining were partially obscured for the same reason but seemed only of minor interest and the Count did not even offer comment on them. Many were apparently the accoutrements of lost or forgotten ritual significance. I maintained a close watch for any item that bore a passing resemblance to anything known to me or represented in the ancient volume concealed beneath my bed, but none revealed themselves. Once or twice we passed by objects of a more grisly origin, being portions of human anatomy scarcely recognizable as a result of the ravages of Time. In answer to my enquiries, the Count answered only that they were the remains of beings that had been of interest to his forebears but whose significance was not known to him personally. I saw no advantage in pursuing the matter. Of the remaining exhibits I have elected to represent only those of particular interest to the Count for which he had some opinion or information to offer. The objects on this and the following few pages were all in close proximity to one another in a single vaulted chamber.

Dracula This is one object that I shall never part with. It is all that remains of my great-great grandfather who abandoned life more than one thousand years ago by choice. He had tired of the passing centuries, having become the first in the family's tradition of vampirism. He had, however, been introduced to the trait very late in his life. His immortality, therefore, began when he was already very elderly with the result that he enjoyed few of the benefits of extreme longevity but all of the disadvantages. It is far less attractive a proposition if the principal attributes are an eternity of creaking joints, arthritis and senile dementia.

After enduring his lot for a century of two, he became less and less inclined to prolong it and began to seriously consider seeking some release from it. It was not a decision he was able to consider lightly, for, by then, he had ensured the perpetuation of his vampirism by electing to physically introduce the strain to his son, my great grandfather. An act which in contemporary society would be considered extremely bad form, but which in those far off days when supernatural society was an unstructured and primitive affair, was not so regarded.

My great grandfather, however, proved a considerable disappointment to him and seemed to bitterly resent the characteristic he had unwillingly acquired. He devoted his entire life to attempting to undo the legacy bequeathed to him by his father, much to the latter's disgust and dismay. In those days, you see, his vampirism was the only thing that elevated the family above the plethora of petty tribal chieftains and warlords extant at that time.

It was, after all, the era of small tribal groups, one of which was governed by my ancestral family, and survival was a crude and martial affair consisting of an endless round of raids and minor wars. Becoming a vampire was, to my great-great grandfather's way of thinking, the best thing that had happened to the family since they settled on this very crag and built their stronghold here. It offered, in the associations and immortality it represented, a major advantage in particularly uncertain times, and he was anxious to preserve those qualities in perpetuity through his descendants.

When he finally was able to endure the interminable discomfort of his elderly frame no longer, he resolved to do what he could to ensure that his errant son did not surrender, or fail to pass on, the quality that he regarded so highly. In those early days of the family's history, when demigods were all the rage, they elected to worship Sevageth, the serpent God. We now know Sevageth to be no more than a very minor demon, low in the hierarchy of Hades, but at that time he was more active on the face of the Earth and was a fairly impressive entity. My great-great grandfather did a deal with him, exchanging his soul, or what remained of it, for an existence as one of the demon's acolytes. In this way he was able to retain a strong influence over his son to ensure that the latter continued to meet his obligations. The skull here is my great-great grandfather's and the serpent which inhabits it is the man himself. He is now too ancient to be effectual and sleeps out his personal eternity inside its bony citadel. I must admit that, as I had rather forgotten about the old tyrant, it is good to see that he's still around. It is quite comforting to have that kind of family continuity to provide personal links with one's family history and antiquity.

Dracula This unusual skull was the beginning and the end of my father's excursion into necromancy. He had long been interested in this particular Dark Art and had read extensively on the subject. He also had associations with a number of leading exponents in that field and was always very impressed with their efforts – so much so that he assisted them in certain of their professional engagements in order to learn more of their craft. I rather suspect that they indulged him out of respect for his social position and because his patronage was useful to them. Whatever the case, my father acquired quite a fair amount of knowledge of their procedures and techniques and was prone to dabbling in such matters despite his total lack of qualifications in the subject.

For the most part his activities were harmless enough, consisting mainly of animating animal corpses and manipulating lesser spirits. However, regrettably, his ambitions were for greater things than these. His first major experiment had its beginnings when he heard of a young woman who had committed suicide after murdering her lover. Incidentally, the lover had intended to wed her for her inheritance and had already determined to dispose of her in favour of her sister.

Intrigued by the story, and having secured access to her grave, he decided to see whether he could alter the pattern of subsequent events – a project that would daunt fully qualified necromancers. He did, it is true, succeed in animating her corpse but his success was pathetically short-lived. The woman/zombie immediately broke free of his control and slew her sister, before going on the rampage. His attempts to dissolve her form were only partially successful with the result that she wavers between her artificially restored form and her mortal remains. Her lover's spirit was so enraged at the killing of his love – her sister – that his corpse was spontaneously re-animated and came after my father. It was only my father's acquaintances that saved him from an unpleasant end. His lesson learned, he kept these as reminders of his folly.

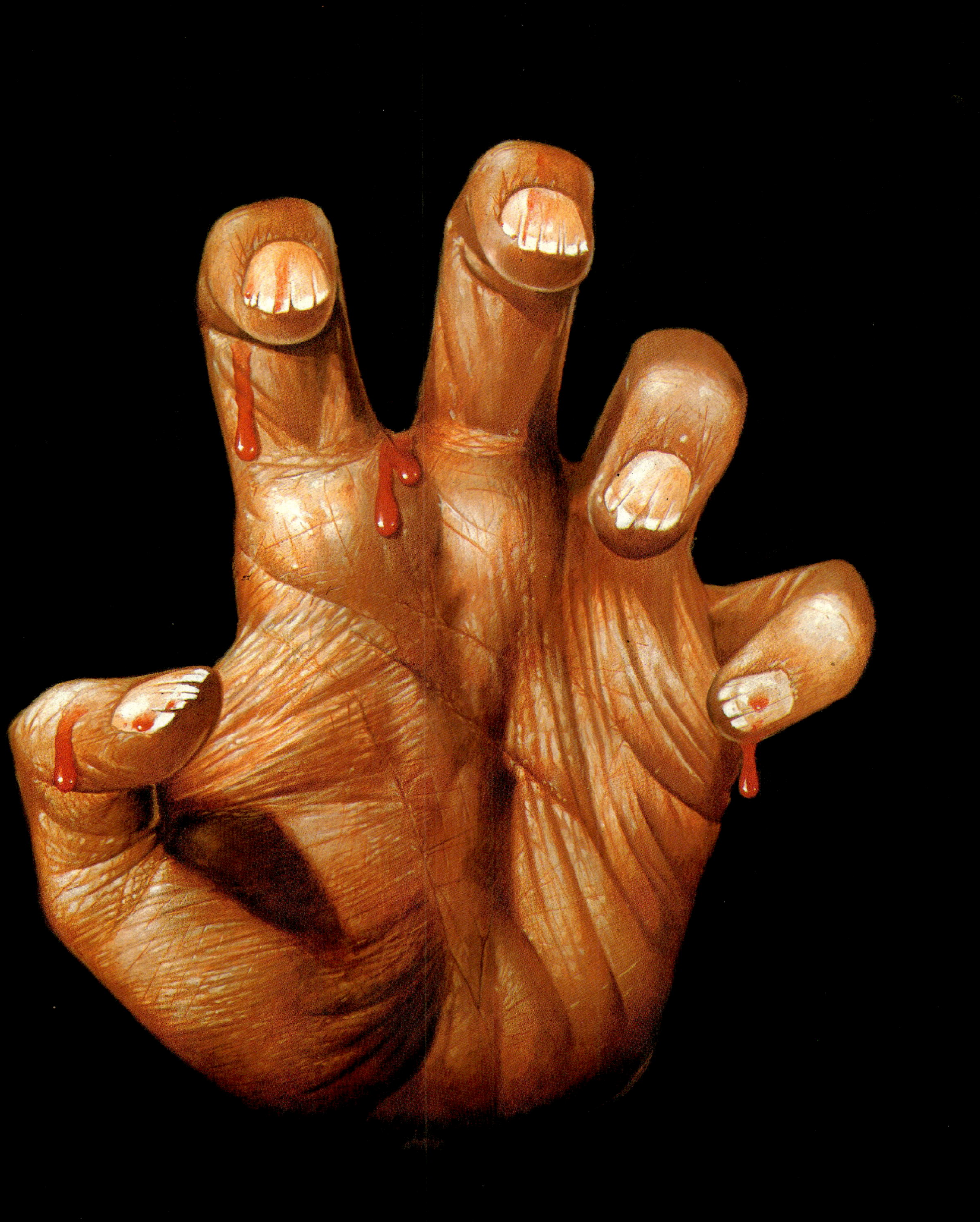

Author's note After passing through many rooms in the museum, we came at last to a great door, stoutly barred and bolted, which was set in the wall of what must have been the original and most ancient portion of this rambling fortress. Outside stood a huge stone sarcophagus of antique design, in the top of which was an aperture covered by a wooden lid. When we stood before this mysterious portal, the Count stepped up to the sarcophagus, removed the lid and reached deep inside. As he drew out his hand, I saw to my absolute horror that it held a slimy, dribbling mass of human eyes which he held before him as he returned to face the door. He produced a large key from beneath his cloak and inserted it in the massive lock. The tumblers clanked back and, after throwing back the huge bolts, he pushed the door open. Inside was utter blackness.

Dracula For me, this is the most welcome part of this place, for this is my refuge from the light. You are privileged indeed to see it; few have had the opportunity. I only permit you this liberty because of your interest and because the guardians herein are more than a match for you should you ever intend me harm. For two of the three these little tidbits are their favourite sweetmeat.

Author's note With that we entered, my heart in my mouth in expectation of what I would see. Inside there was a vast chamber illuminated by a strange greenish glow which revealed a monstrous sight. A gigantic bat and an equally impressive lizard moved ponderously around the form of a beautiful woman hanging in chains.

Dracula There you see one of the fearsome lizards of Hades. It was a gift to my father from Beelzebub himself; it guarded him and now protects me. The bat is the last survivor of a supernatural species no longer to be found in the world; it protects me from influences from the Other Side. The woman is a demon of the Third Order who once intended me harm but proved unequal to the Task. I have succeeded in manipulating certain Dark Forces so that her life is inextricably intertwined with mine. If I am threatened, so is she. As her many powers exceed mine she represents an excellent sentinel for she is as immortal as I am.

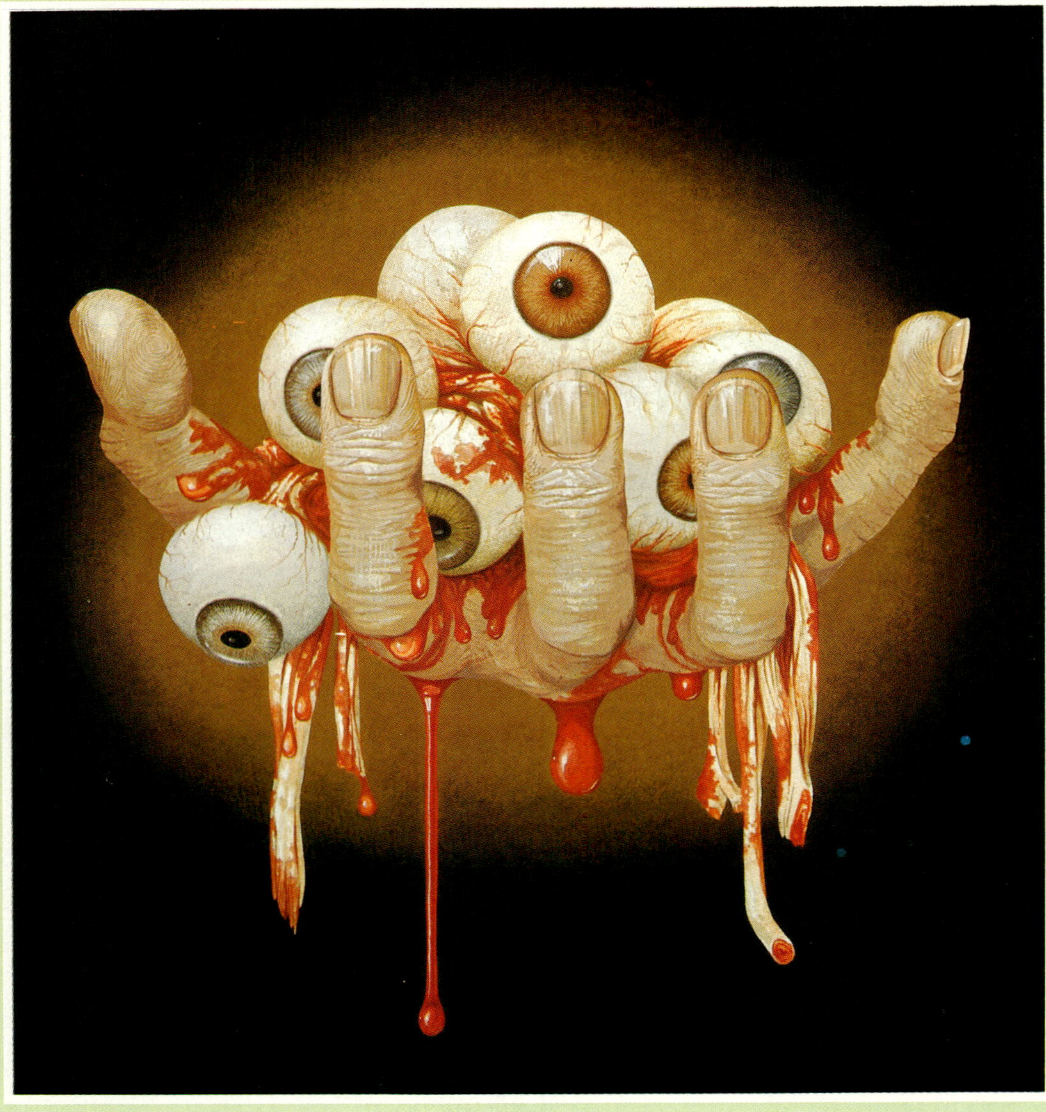

Author's note Although not actually a part of what remains of the Dracula Museum, the item depicted here, which stands in the long dining room of the castle, is, in my opinion, worthy of note. It is also, strangely enough, considering that its appearance is far less terrible than many of the things that I have seen since arriving here, the one object which disturbs me most of all and which suggests that the time has come for me to take my leave of this dreadful place. I had never noticed it before the Count made a point, one evening, of drawing my attention to it. The moment that I laid eyes on it I felt that the danger which has always faced me during my sojourn in this forbidden house became multiplied a thousand-fold.

Dracula This instrument represents one of the most valuable heirlooms to be inherited by me, and not because of the materials of which it is made, nor the skill with which it has been wrought. It was given to me by a close friend of my father's from the other side of the Dark Curtain shortly after his demise, and has served me well on more than one occasion.

Author It is certainly a striking object and excellently made, but I regret that I do not understand its significance.

Dracula I did not expect that you should, for it is not immediately clear what its real function is. It was fashioned by one of the Black Magi who was also a necromancer of the highest standing and a life-long associate of my family. The world beyond the boundaries of Transylvania is a restless place and its curiosity is an ever-increasing threat to the solitude of this land. There are many here who feel the greatest concern as to the future of the land and its inhabitants, particularly those with supernatural associations. It was with this foresight that my benefactor bestowed on me this gift through his affection for the line, of which I am the sole remaining representative.

It is not, as you may believe, a clock to measure the passing of time; it is instead designed to measure levels of life-force. I suppose it could be described as a spiritual barometer. It is useful for me because it can detect and record the presence of mortals and is usually regulated to detect their presence in the vicinity of the castle. As a result, I have sufficient warning, should a group of such being choose to approach the castle, to allow me to make preparations as would be expedient under the circumstances, or at least until I was confident that they meant me no harm. Sadly, its power diminishes with distance and can only register the presence of three or more individuals in close proximity to one another at a given distance. Nevertheless, as I believe that mortals intending to do me harm would be uncertain enough to prefer to approach together, it should be adequate for me.

Author It is a truly remarkable device. Do I infer that its sensitivity can be adjusted to various distances?

Dracula Of course. For example, there lies a small hamlet less than a league from here which contains a sufficient number of mortals for the purpose of a demonstration. I can adjust its mechanism thus . . . and you can see that the face of the instrument is registering their existence. The exquisitely articulated serpents are a teasing reference to my family's old allegiance to Savageth.

Author's note This interlude frightened me very considerably, for I appreciate that my safety here has depended greatly on the Count's lack of awareness of my origins. True, I mean him no harm, and he is probably certain of this, but he has revealed matters to me that I know he would not wish a mortal to know. Indeed, I believe that he, as a supernatural entity, is strictly bound by the laws of that realm not to reveal much of what has now been made known to me. Perhaps I am not in danger after all, for I am not certain, after the circumstances through which I have passed, that I am still a mortal. If this were the case I would pose no threat to him and perhaps he knows more of my true state than I do myself, and feels, therefore, at liberty to speak as we have done. If not, however, my situation is grave indeed, for if he should discover that I am still of the physical world, his position in supernatural society will be most seriously undermined. I fear his displeasure greatly, having no wish to be subjected to the powers that are undoubtedly his to command.

The next day, when he was securely esconced within his catacomb, I elected to return to the place where the device he had demonstrated to me lay. To my horror, I saw that its face clearly indicated the presence of a mortal, and was certain that it was I. Who else would be abroad in this terrible house? I could only conclude that he had, from idle curiosity or the stirring of mistrust, reset the device to record its impressions of the immediate vicinity. I could not alter its setting without alerting the Count, yet its present setting was equally fatal to me. My time is drawing near.

THE RACE FOR LIFE

Something in my relationship with the Count has altered in the last few days and I feel distinctly uncomfortable in his presence. He seems restless and abstracted; often he fixes me with a singularly disturbing stare as he speaks. He has, admittedly, always been somewhat aloof, but was unfailingly cordial and solicitous. Now, however, he does not afford me the time for conversation as he has done since my arrival and I see little of him. At times I am aware of his presence and feel him watching me from a distance. The atmosphere within these unhallowed walls is more sinister than I have felt before and my sleep is disturbed by truly terrible nightmares from which I awake in a state of great anxiety.

I spend long hours in ardent study of the book I carried with me from the herbalist's shop, which now seemed so far away in time and space. Though I have read it over and over again, and learned its formulae for defence against Dracula's ilk by heart, I still fear that my protection is inadequate. His own sinister powers are not the only fearsome forces abroad in this dire realm and I fear that my every defence will ultimately prove inadequate. At times I think he must be aware of the silver crucifix beneath my shirt and the sprigs of rosemary in my pocket, but I dare not be without them.

Each night, without fail, I draw out the indicate patterns of the Alpha Palladium around my bed, but still I feel unsafe. Often, when I wake fevered and bathed in perspiration from some awful presentiment, I think I can detect the furtive scurryings of nameless things around the perimeter of the mystic circle, as though they seek ceaselessly for some chink in my occult redoubt.

The Count is noticeably less willing to converse with me and spends much of his time elsewhere in this rambling pile. He seems tense and restless; I frequently spy him pacing the gloomy corridors, oblivious of me, or staring with intense concentration from one of the upper windows. I am afraid that the enchantments which previously assured my safety might be wearing thin through constant application. Some of the herbal ointments appear to have given me acne.

Much of my time is now spent deliberating on all I have learned of the Count and his extraordinary environment, but the more I peruse the notes I have taken, the more I wish I had asked. There are so many questions in my mind which have yet to be resolved. Where, for example, does he get his clothes, for they seem in fine repair given their apparent antiquity? I know almost as little of the 'man' himself as I did prior to my arrival at the castle and certainly have gained no revelationary insights into his habitat.

I still have felt no hunger or thirst since my arrival with my guide from the graveyard but neither have I lost any weight. Thank God that I have no need of a diet for I could be no more abstemious than I am at present. My brain, however, does seem thinner and I find concentration increasingly difficult. I am torn between my hunger for further information from my supernatural host and the growing desire to return to my own sphere and time. However, I have no idea how this may be achieved for there is no clue in the occult volume I consult so frequently.

The worst of it is the wretched bats, which seem to have increased in numbers to quite a remarkable degree. They are to be found everywhere: hanging from the ceilings of rooms and passages or hurtling out of the darkness to batter against my windows at night. They are unable to penetrate my protective circle while I lie in my bed, but I am very conscious of their flutterings as they hover overhead. Their eyes gleam redly in the candlelight in a particularly malevolent fashion as I read or make notes in my journal and I am growing to detest them vehemently.

I also am beginning to have difficulty in discerning between waking reality and my fevered dreams. Of the latter I have been experiencing a series of them in which the Count plays an increasingly prominent part. At first I was only dimly aware of his presence, but, as the nights passed, I saw him more frequently and more clearly. Initially he was only to be spied hovering on the outer fringe of my sensibility, a dark shape whose features were indistinct. Only my familiarity with his movements and posture led me to recognize him. Before long, I was able to glimpse his face more fully and all the time he was watching me with a curious and unsettling intentness.

As each night passed, he seemed nearer and more vividly portrayed, carrying with him an aura of evil which also grew in intensity. I began to dread seeing him during the evenings and even, for the first time, began to sense his existence during the days when he was incarcerated deep in the black and brooding bowels of the cellars. I soon had no doubts that the truce between us arising from my recourse to the Black Arts for protection was in greater jeopardy as each day passed.

The very air of the castle seemed charged with supernatural tension, as though unknown forces were gathering in the darkness of this God-forsaken land. I was ever more aware of my lonely isolation in a world to which I could never be more than a tolerated but uninvited guest, and yet I had no other choice for the powers that brought me here gave me no clue as to how I might employ them in order to return to the world of the living. In any case, I could not even be certain that I was not myself now one of the undead; had I not observed my own corpse lying blank-eyed on my bed? Even so, I knew that this could not be entirely the case, for otherwise I would be a legitimate inhabitant in this ethereal realm.

At times the Count has seemed reluctant to speak with me, and fixes me with a cruel and penetrating gaze as if to search my very soul for the answer to the question which I fear is in his mind.

Matters took a distinct turn for the worse when, on one of the now rare evenings I shared the same room as the Count, I stumbled and, to prevent a fall, grabbed wildly at one of the hanging tapestries on the wall, and in doing so tore away the nail of my forefinger. The blood welled from the injury as I gritted my teeth and pulled away the damaged cuticle. On turning back to continue my conversation with my host, the words I had intended to speak remained unspoken as I caught sight of his face. His eyes were wide and tinged with a ruddy glow and he was frozen into immobility as he stared fixedly at my injured hand.

I looked at my throbbing hand in some puzzlement at his reaction, then back at him. 'It is a trivial wound and of little consequence,' I replied, a trifle flattered at his seeming concern. To my surprise he threw himself to his feet, stared with terrible concentration into my eyes, then, pulling his cloak around him, strode soundlessly from the room. I stood there, bewildered and uncertain of how I had offended him, for there was an indignant anger in his expression. I walked slowly back to my chamber deep in thought, nursing my injury and ducking bats in an absent-minded manner.

I entered my room and made my way to the bed where I sat, my hand in my lap, and tried to imagine what might have disturbed him so profoundly. My contemplations were interrupted by some commotion beyond the circle of light cast by the candleabra beside the bed, and I looked up in annoyance. To my alarm, I saw a dark, writhing shape near the door, and grabbing the candlestick raised it above my head in order to determine what it was. I gave an involuntary cry as the flickering light was reflected back at me from hundreds of tiny, bead-bright eyes, clustered together in a scintillating mass. I realized quite swiftly that they stared out from the leathery, furry faces of a great number of bats, all hanging together from a shelf on the wall.

I had never seen them behave in such a fashion before and found it somewhat disturbing. I then noticed that they did not seem to be staring at me, but that their attention was directed to a lower part of my anatomy. Perplexed, I looked down at myself to see what could be fascinating them in this way. It was then I noticed that the blood from my finger was still flowing and had seeped over the other hand with which I had been cradling it. As I too looked at the splash of crimson, I caught the singular, slightly metallic smell of it, more strongly than I remember ever noticing before. Suddenly, in a flash of terrible realization, I knew what had so unsettled the Count. Blood! Living Blood!

In that instant I knew with dreadful certainty that my fate was sealed. Though it had never been a subject of discussion, I now understood that my very presence in this supernatural environment implied that I, myself, was not mortal, that I was a legitimate inhabitant here. Perhaps the Count's growing distance with me had been

***Above:* A huge and dismal cloud swept over the sky, shutting out the light and the echo of ghostly hoofbeats reverberated in my heart. As I watched, the spectre of Death thundered overhead.**

***Right:* The blood froze in my very veins as I found myself staring into the ghastly, maddened eyes of the Beast. A nightmare wind howled around me as I felt Life being torn from my frail body.**

the result of clues I had inadvertently left for him. I had never paused to consider how extraordinary it was that he appeared to be quite at ease with me – someone who was the very antithesis of his existence. Now I knew; he had been given no reason to suppose otherwise, for was I not here in the land of the undead, where no mortal could be?

Panic gripped me in its icy fingers and I fought for breath in the face of my lungs' paralysis. I looked again, wide-eyed, to where the chittering, seething mass of bats had hung in the corner, afraid to lower the lamp in case they launched themselves at me through the ensuing darkness. But, to my surprise, the chamber was empty, though I could not surmise how they had passed out of the room. I placed the candelabra beside the bed, lay back and with my heart pounding in my breast and considered earnestly how I might escape whatever fate I now felt sure was being planned for me.

My mystic defences could only delay the results of a concerted effort by whatever supernatural forces were at the Count's command; my own knowledge and abilities would certainly be no match for such infernal powers. I turned again to the worn, leather-bound volume concealed under the mattress and began searching with mounting frustration for some hint of hope.

After some time spent fruitlessly flicking through the pages, my eyes eventually alighted on a portion that I could not recollect having sighted before. It read: 'Harken ye that would be Travellers, for though thy Going may be laboured, thy Returning is more Troubled yet. Fasten thy Lifeline on some unyielding rock, that thou shalt draw upon it to speed thy Homecoming. A Traveller oweth a Great Debt to the Horseman, for he passeth through a domain where a dire Toll is due but had not been paid. If thou would Return, Deny the Darkness and draw upon thy Cord, but beware that no part of thee is left along the Road.'

Try though I did, I could not interpret this passage, but felt convinced that hidden therein lay my salvation. I read it again and again, all the while feeling that my safety ebbed away like a retreating tide. I saw that my presence here was now an affront to the very natural laws of this soulless world, and that the rage of my host was the least that I must escape. Every object in this land was my enemy and the very air seemed resentful and malevolent. I knew that I would have to flee immediately for my life, indeed, for my very soul.

I could wait no longer, and clutching the book to my breast, sprang immediately from the bed, opened the door, and fled down the passageway to the back stairs. How I did not break my neck I shall never know, for I scarcely recall my headlong flight down the study steps. However it was achieved, I found myself out in the chill air. Behind me the great black mass of the castle towered malignantly, as if crouching to spring upon me. I gasped desperately, then hurled myself forward once more, aware only of my wild panic to leave this place far behind. All the while I felt as though Dracula was at my shoulder, those fearful eyes reddened in anticipation of a dreadful, final lunge. The blood thundered in my ears with the extreme effort and my chest heaved as it struggled to extract some nourishment from the diseased air of this awful terrible land.

Eventually I could continue no longer, and fell to my knees in utter exhaustion, the bile rising in my throat from the killing effort. I do not know how long I lay there on the stinking, slimy earth, but eventually my wits returned to me and I began to consider my position more calmly. I had no doubt that the initiative would not remain with me much longer, and I must embark upon some considered course of action immediately. I thought again of the passage in the book and strove to identify some clue as to its meaning. What 'lifeline' could it be referring to? and what 'rock' could be the anchorage for that line?

As I deliberated, I suddenly became aware of the pounding of hooves that seemed to penetrate the earth itself. I drew up my legs until I was as small as I could make myself, and quivered in terror at this unexpected sound. Then the pale dawn light was blotted out as if by a huge cloud and I looked up in terrified anticipation. There, sweeping up from the dim horizon thundered a gigantic horse, blacker than night, and surmounted by a horrible spectre that I knew was Death itself. In one ghastly instant I knew that I was lost. A shrieking filled my ears and an icy pain gripped my heart as I found myself staring directly into the maddened, insane eyes of the beast. A nightmare wind screamed about me and I felt the life being torn from my body and knew that I was paying the Toll and settling my debt to the Horseman.

Suddenly, unbidden, the image of my dear wife, whom I had so cruelly forsaken, sprang vividly into my mind and I felt both love and sorrow surge through my tortured mind. At once the wind ceased. Miraculously, the horrible spectre was gone and I realized that, unwittingly, I had found the Lifeline to which the ancient tome referred. I fell to my knees, rears flooding my eyes as the horror ebbed from my heart.

Though I was safe for the present, I knew that I could only have enraged the ghastly forces of this world still further, and that they would soon beset me once more. I stood up and looked about me, and saw that I was surrounded by great rocks that seemed to rise to the limits of the sky. I searched for some passage between them, and spied a section illuminated by an indistinct glow. I ran towards it and caught sight of a crevice through which there streamed a harsh light. Forcing my way through, I found myself standing at the edge of an unending desert, a sea of sand that stretched to infinity. Tears sprang once again to my eyes for in my foolish hope I had somehow expected to see before me a more familiar world: my own.

I felt as though my mind was surrendering to the insanities which I had been surrounded by for so long. Wild emotions surged within me and fleeting visions beset my inner eye. I fell to my knees in the coarse sand, feeling its heat scorching my flesh. Terrible images flickered at the edges of my vision and I felt myself falling. buffeted by all manner of hellish winds. The heat burned into my eyes and I felt a thirst unlike any I had experienced. Then there was silence and I opened my eyes to see what had become of me. To my horror I found myself totally unable to move: I was imprisoned in the scorching sands. Only my head lay exposed to the blazing sun and my tongue swelled and cracked within my parched mouth.

My vision began to blur as the murderous blast of the sun began to evaporate the moisture of my eyes and dry them to pale, sightless orbs. At least I would be spared the horror of watching the waiting birds swoop down to pluck

Powerful forces plucked at me as I fell to my knees in the coarse sand. Then to my horror I found I was unable to move and opened my eyes to find myself imprisoned in the burning grip of the desert while high above whirled black and sinister shapes.

them from their orbits. As I awaited the jagged lances of agony that must surely strike, my misery began mercifully to subside. Perhaps I had endured all that my frail mortal body and mind was capable of tolerating. I began the long, slow and gentle drift into death, my consciousness filled with little but yearning for my stolen future, and central to it all was the fragile image of my wife. She stole softly into my terminal reverie. At first I was hardly aware that I held her in my mind at all, but gradually, she moved into focus with astonishing clarity. 'My lifeline, my lifeline, my lifeline'. The words hummed like a dirge in my baked skull and some small, insistant spark deep in me flared up. Though my arms were imprisoned in the grainy oven, I reached out to her with a sudden, blazing rush of longing, and her hands pushed outwards to meet me.

A deafening cachophany of hideous shrieks buffeted me and I was plummeting through the same endless void that had opened before me many times before, aeons ago. I felt hands and claws clutching at me, furiously tearing my clothes and tender flesh as I spun crazily through the darkness, moving neither up nor down. Then the blackness swept in on me, blinding and suffocating me and I knew no more.

For what I knew were generations, I floated – deaf, dumb and blind – in the utter nothing that preceded creation. I was dimly aware that elemental forces moved in the void, ordering themselves, shaping themselves as things that were yet to come. I was forgotten, perhaps I too did not yet exist and might never do. I was not important. There are no such things as priorities if Time does not exist. Nothingness is complete unto itself, and I felt complete.

Then abruptly, Time began, and with that I ceased to be a limitless eternity and was given movement through the void. With movement I gained direction, with direction I gained velocity, with velocity I acquired a termination and suddenly there was also light.

My eyes flickered open and I found myself gazing up at the face of my wife. Beside her stood my valet, and both were staring at me with expressions of horror. My wife gave a soft cry and collapsed abruptly, like a house of cards, as the valet tried belatedly to break her fall. Before I could raise myself from the bed to assist him, something made me turn my head to look out of the window. For a brief instant I thought I saw my own face far out in the darkness, turning away from me. Then it was gone like the fading remnants of a vivid dream and I sat up to swing my legs off the bed in order to help in lifting my wife from the floor where she lay unconscious.

I sat with her until she recovered, feeling tired and weak myself and grateful for the opportunity to rest. My mind swam with a disturbing kaleidoscope of impressions and half remembered images. I could not recall what I had done or where I had last been since leaving for London in pursuit of a little frequented herbalist's shop. Disconnected fragments drifted through my imagination, fragments that seemed disturbingly real but were filled with unimaginable horror.

Later that night, once my wife had fully recovered and I had managed to convince here that I was very much alive – though why she had felt convinced otherwise still eluded me – I returned to my bedchamber and prepared to sleep. I remained however, very much awake and in a state of growing tension for I began to feel convinced that the insane visions were unmistakeably stamped with the hallmark of reality, nightmarish though they certainly were. I concentrated on trying to isolate each one separately and fit them together like some immensely complex jigsaw puzzle.

Fragment by fragment they came together and I wrote down each episode as I identified it, ordering them as best I could. The picture that emerged filled me with horror and apprehension for it portrayed circumstances in which no sane man should play or have played a part. After some hours I fell into an exhausted and uneasy sleep, haunted by ghastly moods and entities that were no less appalling in the wan, pre-dawn light seeping in through the window.

When I awoke my mind was clearer and calmer as I read through the scribblings of the night; I recalled many of the fragments of what I now knew to be actual experiences, that had been omitted from this most extraordinary history. I stared out of the window somewhat numbly, unaware of the view outside but lost in the implications of my supernatural escapade. Certain episodes, notably the indeterminate time I remained at Count Dracula's castle, were absolutely clear in my recollection and I was able to record, verbatim, my conversations with him.

I remembered too, the passage in the book now submerged in the burning sands of that distant and unearthly desert, that had provided me with the vital key without which my soul would have perished or been committed to a hellish eternity. In the days that followed, I spent my time refining the account I have made, filling in missing fragments and correcting misrememberances. I could not, however, shake off the feeling that all was not yet finally resolved. Vague fears and a constant uneasiness plagued me, waking and sleeping, and my physical condition deteriorated sufficiently to be apparent to my patient and considerate wife.

Surely the terrible forces with which I had so foolishly played could not reach out to me still? Surely I was now safe at last? Over and over again, I repeated to myself the conclusion to the passage that was my salvation; 'If thou would Return, Deny the Darkness and draw upon thy Cord, but beware that no part of thee is left upon the Road.' I had repeatedly checked my recollection of the night of my awakening and knew for certain that I had left nothing in that unholy place.

That night, I retired in a state of terrible anxiety. I could not quell my overwhelming sense of dread and dared not extinguish the lamp. The very darkness beyond the window seemed to thicken and acquire substance and the air was chill and suffocating. Buzzings and whisperings appeared to grow in volume as I crouched in fear beside my bed. Suddenly a horrible, blood-chilling thought erupted into my mind. In a vivid instant I saw myself seated on the bed in that far away castle, clutching my wounded hand upon my lap. I looked down at the floor between my feet and stared in disbelief at a small circular shape of gleaming, crimson hue; my blood! My own blood glistened still within that ghastly citadel! A scream of utter despair tore from my throat as I rushed to the window to close it against the terror that I knew awaited me without. A vast and indescribable shape hurtled out of the darkness and wrenched me from life.

The air grew thick and heavy in the room where I lay, and a foul odour began to accumulate. Strange whisperings grew to a clamour as I realized with horror that my ordeal was far from over. I ran to the window but as I did so, a vast and terrible shape hurtled out of the darkness and I knew that I was lost.

It is impossible to know for certain the precise nature of the fate that befell the unhappy author on that last, terrible night, but there is no doubt that it was a singularly messy business. It must also have been particularly noisy, but the rest of the household, that is to say his wife, valet and the below-stairs staff, remained strangely oblivious to the cataclysmic events that were taking place within the walls of the house.

It was not until the next morning that the chambermaid discovered the grisly aftermath. As was customary, she knocked softly at her master's door, and hearing no response, entered bearing a tray of tea and some thin slivers of lightly browned toast. The sight that met her sleepy eyes beggers description, and the shock caused her to drop the tray and dissolve into hysterical shrieks of utter horror. The sound alerted the entire household and the valet, closely followed by the mistress of the house, was first to arrive at her side.

For an unbiased, contemporary account of the scene within it is possible to turn to the official description prepared fairly soon after this interlude by the constabulary, the relevant section of which read as follows:

'The officers arrived at the house to be admitted by the subject's personal valet, and having assured themselves that the mistress of the house was being attended to by the physician who had already arrived, made their way to the bedchamber in question. Even before entering they noted a pungent and noisome odour similar to that prevalent in swineyards, but of a peculiar intensity. Inside the room the air was scarcely breathable, being in addition permeated with an uncommonly powerful sulphurous odour. The carpet near the window was heavily impregnated with still moist blood, later identified as human and the adjacent walls and parts of the ceiling also bore considerable and similar staining.

The severely disarticulated remains of a human body in a state of decay advanced to the point of near liquidity lay beneath the sill of the window, although some portions lay towards the centre of the room. This cadaver was later positively identified as being that of the subject of this investigation. Though the blood was identified in a later forensic examination as being of the same type as that of the subject, it is impossible that this was the case in view of the pronounced disparity between the state of deterioration of the body, and therefore its point of death, and the condition of the blood, which was comparatively fresh.

While the first officer was availing himself of the telephone to summon an ambulance, the second continued his investigation of the room and noted the presence of a bulky folder of handwritten notes, including several sheets which had been scattered about the chamber. These were collected and retained for examination. They were apparently written in the subject's own hand, a fact corroborated by the subject's wife.

In addition, the officer noted the presence, on the window sill and frame, of significant quantities of clear fluid, still moist to the touch. Later examination determined that it was a salivary excretion of unknown, origin. The results of this and other forensic studies will be made available to the coroner's hearing.

While awaiting the arrival of the forensic investigators, the officers continued their investigation outside the subject's window and noted the presence of a depression, several square metres in area, immediately outside and below the aforementioned window. Here the grass and shrubbery were crushed and the soil indented as though having been subject to the pressure of a very considerable weight. The cause was not immediately apparent and has not since been established.

The occupants of the house were questioned at length, but insisted that no disturbance had been noted on the night in question. Despite the fact that the corpse was in such an advanced state of decay, all those questioned, including the mistress of the house, insisted that it had not been there earlier that evening. Indeed all confirmed separately and together, that the subject had been alive and in good health up to some six or seven hours before the discovery of the body by the chambermaid. They have consistently refused to alter this statement despite the evidence of the body's condition.'

Although the investigation continued for some time after this report was made, no satisfactory explanation was offered and the Coroner's Court found a verdict of 'death by misadventure: cause unknown'. The constabulary did, however, make a further visit to the room but no new evidence came to light and the case was officially closed. The papers taken in evidence were eventually returned to the author's wife.

Some months later, however, the lady was committed to an asylum for the mentally insane where she remained until her death less than a year later. She insisted to the end that her husband was still alive and was depending on her for assistance of some kind, and that she was in regular communication with him. She was committed against her will as she declared that communication could only take place in the room in which his body had been discovered.

Later occupants of the house have stated that the room is unusable as it has proved impossible, to this day, to dispose of the foul odour that pervades it. The editor, on being invited to examine the room, found this to be so, and also acquired the papers, from which this account has been taken, from the present occupants of the house who found them concealed in the attic. As there were no surviving relatives of their author or his wife to lay claim to them, the editor elected to prepare them for this edition.

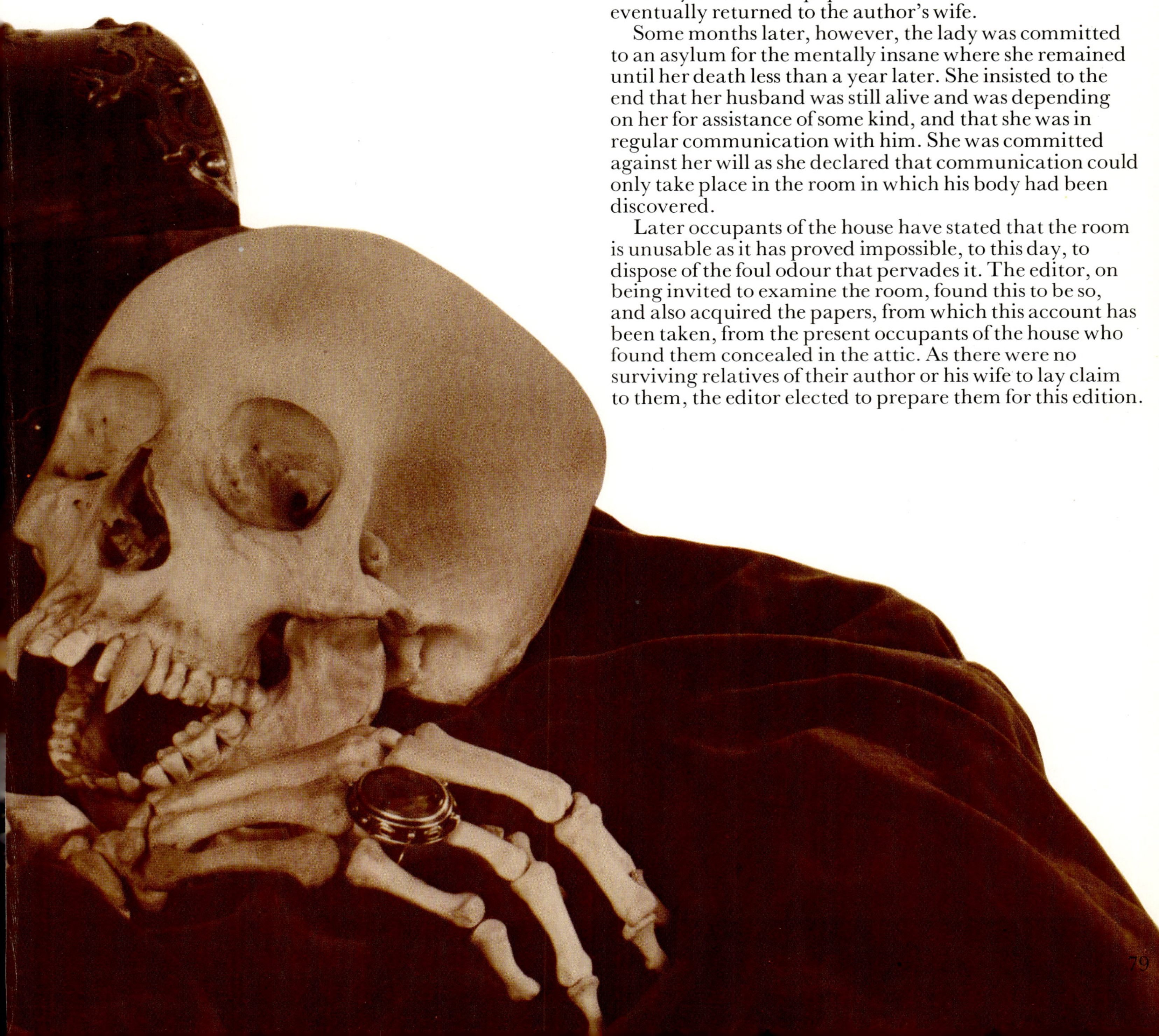

ACKNOWLEDGMENTS

The publishers wish to thank the following individuals and organizations for their kind permission to reproduce the illustrations in this book:

Artist Partners: (Lyn Mitchell) 72; Norma: (Segrelles) 12; Prieto 25, 39; David Lewis Management: (Alun Hood) 14; Chris Moore; 71; Sarah Brown Agency: (Nick Fox) 57, (Alan Senior) 11; Young Artists: (Jim Burns) 17, 20, 33, 53, (Gordon Crabbe) 19, 29, (Les Edwards), Title pages, 7, 9, 15, 22, 26/27, 30, 31, 37, 41, 42, 43, 44, 45, 47, 49, 60, 61, 63, 64, 65, 66, (Phillip Hood) Title verso, (Stuart Hughes) 69, (Terry Oakes) 34/35, 38, 50, 54, 59, 73, 75, 77, (George Smith) Half-title, 21, 67. Estelle for her bones, 78/79.